THE
EXCEPTIONAL
PRESENTER

A PROVEN FORMULA TO OPEN UP! AND OWN THE ROOM

Timothy J. Koegel

To purchase additional copies of *The Exceptional Presenter*
or learn more about the author visit
www.theexceptionalpresenter.com

The Exceptional Presenter

A Proven Formula to OPEN UP! and Own the Room

By Timothy J. Koegel

Published by: Timothy J. Koegel
The Koegel Group
Washington, DC 20004
www.theexceptionalpresenter.com

Third printing

Illustrations by: Vanesa Ardaya, Paul Koegel and Tim Koegel
Cover design and inside layout: Ad Graphics, thebookproducer.com
Cover photo credit: Masterfile, www.masterfile.com
Printed by: Central Plains Book Manufacturing, www.centralplainsbook.com, (877) 278-2726

ISBN: 0-9720506-0-4

DEDICATION

To Amy, Kaitlyn and Marty with whom I am grateful and honored to share life's journey.

To Mom and Dad. I am forever thankful for your love, your support and your encouragement. You taught me that faith, family and community are what truly matter in life. And although Dad has passed, his love of life, sense of humor, uplifting spirit and artistic talent shall remain forever in the hearts and minds of those who knew him.

This illustration by Paul Koegel

TABLE OF CONTENTS

ACKNOWLEDGMENTS

A special thanks to all of those who helped bring *The Exceptional Presenter* to fruition.

To Erik Lokkesmoe, a talented and versatile Washington, DC speechwriter. Your expertise, perspective and sense of humor were invaluable in developing both the flow and the feel of this book.

To Rick Buehner, you are a true friend and marketing guru. Your sage advice and lucid feedback kept me on course.

To the artistic skills of illustrator Vanessa Ardaya.

To Jim and Barbara Weems of Ad Graphics. Your guidance, direction and patience took the pain out of publishing.

To Cheryl Drake for your expertise in editing *The Exceptional Presenter*.

To Melody Morris and the professionals at Central Plains Book Manufacturing.

From the Author...

The *Exceptional Presenter* is designed to provide the essential skills, techniques and strategies necessary for you to present yourself and your ideas at an exceptional level, to any audience, in any venue.

You can read it on a flight from DC to Dallas, on the treadmill or in small doses at night before bed. It reads more like a presentation than a textbook, including stories, examples, bullet points, exercises, performance tracking, note pages and practice charts.

Consistently exceeding an audience's expectations is a hallmark of all exceptional presenters. Therefore, use this book often, especially before major presentations, as a Coach/Mentor to inspire you to rise to the occasion.

The format of the book is designed to be concise, focusing only on the core information and allowing you to use it as a quick reference. Highlight it. Mark it up. Document your observations and communication experiences.

Make this book your personal presentation diary and carry it with you on your journey to becoming exceptional!

Tim Koegel

CHAPTER ONE

The Exceptional Presenter

B ecoming an exceptional presenter seems to be a Herculean task. There's a lot to remember. Say this. Move that. Speak up. Look at the audience. Don't fidget. You leave the meeting wondering, "Did I connect? Was I clear? Was that guy sleeping, or was he praying for my presentation to end?"

There are a lot of "experts" out there who will give you all the answers. Type into a leading Internet search engine the words, "public speaking" and you'll get 2,350,000 hits. After a while it all seems to sound the same.

The formula you are about to learn is designed to take the mystery and the misery out of presenting. We will break down the art of presenting into a series of skills. Then you will learn a systematic approach to mastering each skill.

The objectives of this book are straightforward and achievable:

1) Share a proven formula that will enable you to communicate at an exceptional level, in any venue, to any audience.

2) Provide a practice method to help you develop skills that will not fail under pressure.

3) Serve as your personal diary to document your improvement.

No two people are positioned exactly the same when it comes to presentation style, comfort level or expertise. Every presenter and every presentation is unique. But one thing we can all share is the cascade of benefits that come from acquiring exceptional skills.

The benefits will affect every aspect of your life. Your presentation skill level will affect your income and career track. It will affect your personal relationships and your ability to lead and persuade others. It will affect what job you land and what reputation you build.

What Makes a Presenter Exceptional?

Write down the names of two exceptional presenters, living or deceased. Select a media personality, an athlete, a politician, a professor or perhaps a business or religious leader.

What characteristics make them exceptional? List four characteristics or traits for each person.

Exceptional presenter #1: _____

Characteristics: _____

    _____

    _____

    _____

Exceptional presenter #2: _____

Characteristics: _____

    _____

    _____

    _____

In the last fifteen years I've asked more than 6000 workshop participants to fill out the form you just filled out. The results open the door to understanding what makes people stand out as presenters. The results have enabled me to develop a formula that turns average presenters into exceptional presenters.

Our next step is to discover what it means to OPEN UP! and Own the Room.

OPEN UP!

OPEN UP! is an acronym representing the six characteristics shared by exceptional presenters. The secret is not just knowing the characteristics, but understanding how to incorporate them into your presentation style.

The Exceptional Presenter is:

ORGANIZED

Exceptional presenters take charge! They look poised and polished. They sound prepared. You get the sense that they are not there to waste time. Their goal is not to overwhelm, but to inform, persuade, influence, entertain or enlighten. Their message is well structured and clearly defined.

PASSIONATE

Exceptional presenters exude enthusiasm and conviction. If the presenter doesn't look and sound passionate about his or her topic, why would anyone else be passionate about it? Exceptional presenters speak from the heart and leave no doubt as to where they stand. Their energy is persuasive and contagious.

ENGAGING

Exceptional presenters do everything in their power to engage each audience member. They build rapport quickly and involve the audience early and often. If you want their respect, you must first connect.

NATURAL

An exceptional presenter's style is natural. Their delivery has a conversational feel. Natural presenters make it look easy. They appear comfortable with any audience. A presenter who appears natural appears confident.

UNDERSTAND YOUR AUDIENCE

Exceptional presenters learn as much as they can about their audience before presenting to them. The more they know about the audience, the easier it will be to connect with them.

PRACTICE

Those who practice improve. Those who don't, don't. Exceptional skills <u>must</u> become second nature.

Practice is the most important part of the improvement process. If your delivery skills are second nature, they will not fail under pressure.

There are hundreds of opportunities every day to practice the skills in this book. The only thing you need is the desire to practice. Most people never practice. If they do, it's on their way to present a proposal, interview for a job, deliver a keynote presentation or sell an idea to their boss. The time to practice is not in "live," win or lose situations. The time to practice is during your normal daily routines, when habits can be formed and mistakes are not costly.

Throughout this book I will highlight daily practice opportunities. You will be surprised at how convenient and how easy practicing can be.

Own the Room

Own the room is a term describing an actor who is so completely into character that he walks on stage with total confidence. He owns the room.

Owning the room is what will happen for you once you have developed an OPEN communication style. You will present with total confidence and maintain the highest level of professionalism, even in the most challenging circumstances. You will hold yourself accountable for the success or failure of your presentations. And you will do whatever it takes to ensure that your audience understands and remembers your message.

Chapters four through nine show you specifically how to incorporate these six characteristics (OPEN UP!) of the world's top presenters into your style. You'll learn in detail how to OPEN UP! and Own the Room.

Exceptional Presentation Skills Win Elections

Whether you agreed or disagreed with him, President Bill Clinton was and still is an excellent example of where exceptional presentation skills can take your career. Ask his 1992 and 1996 opponents, George H. Bush and Bob Dole, if presentation skills played a role in the outcome of those two Presidential elections. Both Bush and Dole were highly intelligent, both were World War II veterans, and both were scandal free. They each brought vast experience to their campaigns. But despite their credentials, neither could match the presentation skills of William Jefferson Clinton.

From the first question of his first presidential debate, Bill Clinton "owned the room." When the first question was directed his way, candidate Clinton walked toward the lady who had asked the question. He squared his shoulders to her. He looked her straight in the eye and asked her to repeat her name. Then he answered her question. He was connecting from the opening bell.

In the days following presidential debates, I will survey participants in my workshops to find out how much they remembered from the debate. Typically they don't remember much. They'll remember a one-liner or a gaffe. They'll remember questions related to a topic near and dear to their hearts (the environment, education, nuclear arms, Social Security). But despite the fact that they remembered little of what was said, they always had an opinion as to who won. "He carried himself like a president." "He was unflappable." "He connected with me." "He seemed more knowledgeable."

The first televised debate took place in 1960 between candidates Richard Nixon and John Kennedy. The polls following the debate were telling. The majority of people who listened to the debate on the radio thought Nixon had won. The majority of those who watched the debate on TV thought Kennedy had won.

Kennedy looked sharp. He looked fresh. His presence was charismatic. Richard Nixon, on the other hand, had not shaved prior to the debate. His five o'clock shadow caused him to appear tired and a bit haggard. In a video taken prior to the debate Nixon could be heard saying, "Guess I should have shaved." That was the understatement of the evening.

Nixon also decided not to use make-up because he overheard Kennedy refusing make-up. He did not know that Kennedy had been made up earlier in the evening.

Flash to the 1992 debate between President George H. Bush, Bill Clinton and Ross Perot. During the town hall debate President Bush glanced at his watch several times. Years later in an interview with Jim Leherer, President Bush admitted that glancing at his watch reinforced a mistaken general perception that his heart wasn't 100% into the campaign.

In the first Election 2000 debate it was Al Gore's behavior that damaged his effectiveness. He sighed loudly when he disagreed with then Governor George W. Bush. He interrupted and rolled his eyes repeatedly. His behavior overshadowed anything he had to say about domestic or foreign issues.

The highlight of John Kerry's 2004 run for the White House and the worst performance of the Bush campaign happened the night of the first Presidential debate.

The normally mechanical Kerry appeared relaxed and conversational. His posture at the lectern was commanding. He seemed well prepared. He looked and sounded like someone who could be President.

President Bush appeared tired. He leaned on his lectern throughout the debate. Frequent facial expressions suggested that the President was agitated or frustrated with his opponent, yet the President did not verbally counter punch. Excessive filler, ums and uhs, combined with the overuse of certain phrases led to the impression that the President was armed with twelve minutes of information for a ninety-minute debate. The President's six to eight point poll lead disappeared.

A much more prepared, passionate and commanding President Bush showed up for debates two and three. He was able to regain his momentum and win the election.

The lesson from Election 2004: Every presentation counts! Never let your competition back in the game by turning in a less than exceptional performance.

CHAPTER TWO

It's Not Where You Start It's Where You Finish

There has never been a more important time to possess exceptional presentation skills. We've moved from an economy of high paying jobs and breakneck business expansion to an economy where job opportunities have been severely reduced and businesses face stiff competition at every level.

Business leaders tell me that instead of competing against two or three firms, they now face four to six firms proposing for the same assignment. The margin of error has vanished. Missteps and missed opportunities are costly.

Both the 2004 GMAC Corporate Recruiters Survey and the 2004 Wall Street Journal MBA Rankings listed communication skills as the #1 hiring criteria for MBA students.

People who present at an exceptional level maintain a distinct competitive advantage in winning new business and securing the best jobs. In an unforgiving economy their advantage becomes even more pronounced.

A client in San Francisco takes full advantage of his presentation prowess. His strategy is to force his competition into a beauty contest, where he and his competitors present their capabilities and solutions to the prospect. As he puts it, "Most of my competitors don't like to present, they don't know how to prepare, and most are not good presenters. If I can present to the prospect at any stage in the selection process, I have a good chance of winning the assignment."

Do not discount your potential as a presenter.

I've helped thousands of people communicate more powerful messages to their prospects, voters, employers, investors and the media. I've consulted at the White House, in boardrooms, at business schools and CEO boot camps, from Capitol Hill to Silicon Valley. Wherever I go, or whomever I work with, one fact remains consistent: **No matter what your skill level — no matter what your presentation comfort level — you can become exceptional.**

Take Lee, a design and construction specialist in Dallas. Lee initially rated himself a 3 on a scale of 1-10 (10 being the best). He now consistently presents in the 8-9 range, and he looks forward to presentations rather than trying to avoid them.

Or Carol, an investment advisor in Indianapolis. Nervousness nearly caused Carol to pass out any time she rose to speak. Carol now presents with poise and confidence. Her nerves are no longer a barrier to her communication efforts, and her speaking skills are creating new sources of revenue and relationships.

Even the greatest speaker of the 20th Century, Winston Churchill, had to overcome fears and limitations. Still, he said, "There are only a few things in life from which I derive intense pleasure, speaking is not one of them!"

The Exceptional Presenter is not a complex book. It's not rocket science. Rather, it's rocket fuel — some helpful tips designed to lift your skills to new heights. In fact, you will learn that presenting is quite basic. Once we break down the components of presenting, mastering those components becomes as easy as practice and repetition.

Do not underestimate the power of your delivery.

Dr. Albert Mahrabian, a professor at UCLA, conducted research to find out what determines our communication impact. The results of his study are essential to our understanding of presentation effectiveness.

His studies revealed that:

7% **of our impact is determined by the words we use.**

38% **of our impact is determined by our voice: how confident and comfortable we sound.**

55% **of our impact is determined non-verbally: our appearance, posture, gestures and movement, eye contact and facial expressions.**

Does Dr. Mahrabian's study suggest that our words are not important? No. Our words are critical. The study does, however, highlight the fact that 93% of our communication impact comes from the way we deliver our words.

Do not underestimate how often you use these skills.

Adopt a broader definition of "presentation skills" to include any form of oral communication. I frequently hear the following comment, "I only present once or twice a year. I don't use these skills very often."

That's not true. Keep in mind that every time you speak in public you are a public speaker. Every time you utter a phrase within earshot of another human being, you are making an impression. Even when you listen, your body language is projecting a message back to that person.

Circle the venues in which you have found yourself presenting (speaking or listening):

Sales meetings	Proposals
Staff meetings	Prospecting calls
Voice mail	Job interviews
Networking	Customer service
Phone conversations	Negotiating
Instructing others	Training
Counseling	IPO road shows
Cold calls	Radio or TV appearances
Keynote speeches	Fund raising
Introducing others	Social functions
Team presentations	Client reviews
Product introductions	Banquets
Key account meetings	Casual conversations
Q&A sessions	Brainstorming sessions
Hosting an event	Recruiting
Reading at services	Interviewing candidates
Luncheons	Board meetings
Questioning clients	Mentoring
Selling products	Talking to your children
Updating superiors	Sharing your vision
Coaching	Arguing
Talking with spouse	Debating
Talking with peers	Gossiping
Working convention booths	Teaching

All of the above venues should be included in your new definition of presentations.

I suspect you have multiple circles on the page. If you have only one, you can still benefit from the techniques in this book.

A Cascade of Benefits Awaits the Exceptional Presenter

Get excited about what you can achieve with these skills. The end result of exceptional presentation skills can be seen in the following list of benefits clients have told me they have experienced:

- Build a reputation as THE preeminent authority.

    Dateline: Chicago – A senior manager with a financial services firm was looking to build eminence in the business community for his practice. He pursued opportunities to speak to business groups in Chicago on the topic of corporate fraud. He achieved his goal of building eminence. He also landed several new clients, including one that generated $3.5 million of revenue within fourteen months. The senior manager is now a partner, partly due to his ability to generate new sources of revenue for his firm.

- Leverage your time. Presenting to groups is an efficient way to prospect. Few organizations adopt a strategic approach to this prospecting gold mine.

    Dateline: DC – A client accepts an opportunity to deliver a state-of-the-market presentation to a group of 160 CEOs and CFOs. For 45 minutes, the client had the undivided attention of those executives. They have since conducted business with over a dozen of the attendees. Others have requested follow-up meetings. The resulting revenue will stream in for years. How long would it take to schedule separate meetings with 160 CEOs and CFOs? It would be a difficult task.

- Present with confidence to superiors, peers and subordinates. Most of us spend a significant amount of time communicating. A higher level of communication confidence will spill over to other aspects of our lives.

- Increase your earning potential.

- Conduct results-oriented meetings.

- Win a higher percentage of proposals.

- Become more versitile. The more you can do, the better your chances of staying on the payroll.

- Showcase your story when interviewing.

- Build credibility within your organization.

- Secure lasting relations with clients and customers.

- Project the image and presence of a leader.

- Increase your ability to influence others.

- Enhance marketability. Organizations can't afford to lose exceptional communicators.

- Make strong first impressions.

- Network more effectively.

- Fast track your career.

- Become a rainmaker.

- Excel at leading, inspiring and motivating others.

What other benefits might you derive?

_____

_____

_____

_____

A client from Denver recently told me that in addition to boosting his business, these skills have made him a much better Sunday School teacher. He can see the difference in the attentiveness of his young pupils. His improved skills are making a positive difference in the lives of his clients and his students.

How Are You Positioned as a Presenter?

Experience tells me that 80% of presenters are below average, 10% are average, 5% are good to very good and 5% are exceptional.

The percentage of exceptional presenters can and should be significantly higher. Most presenters never tap their full potential.

Most presenters are below average because they:

- Don't seriously commit to improving.
- Don't attend presentation training.
- Don't videotape and critique their presentation style.
- Don't seek objective feedback from an expert.
- Don't have a system to develop productive habits.
- Don't know how to practice.

They're stuck, and their effectiveness or lack thereof will not change.

Exceptional presenters understand that much of their success is attributable to their superior skills. They're confident in knowing that they maintain a competitive advantage because of their advanced skills. All things being equal (experience, education, knowledge, price, service) the exceptional presenter is more likely to win the proposal, be offered the job, win the election, retain the client, convince the boss or sell the idea.

If you don't think these skills are critical, keep your fingers crossed that your competition has the same attitude. If your competitors understand the impact of these skills, and they reach the exceptional level, they will dominate in competitive situations.

CHAPTER THREE

Present to Win
or
Prepare to Lose

What is the cost of having less than exceptional or poor presentation skills? No one truly knows. Rest assured, if your skills are lacking, you are losing money, handcuffing your ability to land your dream job, damaging your professional image and derailing your career aspirations.

According to the Association of Fraud Examiners, American businesses lost nearly $700 billion to internal fraud in 2004. That's roughly 6% of annual revenue. It's money right out the door.

I'd venture to say that the typical American business loses at least 6% of annual revenue to poor communication skills.

My accounting clients tell me that when a company learns that it's losing 6% of revenue to fraud, the company immediately puts plans in place to stop the bleeding. It's painful to realize that someone is stealing your hard-earned money. "We'll catch the thieves and throw them in jail," they say. "I don't care what it costs to stop these criminals."

By contrast, losing revenue because of poor presentation skills isn't quite as painful. It's easier to ignore. The money never flowed in. You never had it in the first place. So, we say, "Oh, well, that one got away. We'll get the next one."

Every company should establish an accounting ledger for business they've lost due to poor presentation skills. They have budgets for training, development, travel and entertainment. Why not establish a "blown opportunity" budget each fiscal year? "As soon as we've achieved $15 million in revenue that we should have had, we'll do something to beef up the way we communicate our services."

An average presenter's loss is an exceptional presenter's gain.

How Was I to Know? No One Ever Told Me!

*"Advice is seldom welcome.
Those who need it most, like it least."*
Samuel Johnson

How do you know if your presentation skills are lacking? How can you measure your effectiveness if you don't assess your skills? Rarely will someone volunteer honest, pull-no-punches feedback. Most people don't like being the bearer of bad news. On the flip side, most people don't willingly or gracefully accept feedback.

You probably won't hear people say:

- "Jim, your speech was pathetic. I assume you didn't have time to practice."

- "Sue, we appreciate you coming in and boring us to tears."

- "John, I'm curious, have you considered a speech coach?"

- "Of all the speakers we've heard, you are without question, the worst. And we've heard a lot of speakers."

We'd be lucky to hear such comments. If we were lousy, wouldn't we want to know? I'd rather have someone tell me I didn't look prepared, I missed the mark, or that my presentation was boring than have someone pat me on the back and say, "Nice job." A dose of reality can serve as a wake-up call and encourage us to improve the way we present our information.

Seeking feedback from a presentation coach is an excellent way to assess your skills. Make sure the coach uses videotape to provide feedback. The camera doesn't lie. What you see and hear on tape is what your audience sees and hears. A coach will highlight your strengths and bring attention to those skill sets in need of refinement.

A coach will spot tendencies that an untrained person would miss. Most people can tell a good presentation from a bad presentation. But can they pinpoint specific reasons it was good or bad? Can they readily spot body language that is incongruent with the words being spoken? Can they discern vocal variations that cause an audience to disengage? Can they pick up mannerisms that create negative impressions? Probably not. Professional evaluation is essential.

The Cost of Average Illustrated

Dateline: Silicon Valley, CA – Bob Marshall, Silicon Valley legend and CEO of Selby Venture Partners, estimates that 80% of start-up companies die with their funding presentations. The company executives are unable to present their technology in a way that investors understand. In addition, 80% of the CEOs are poor presenters. They don't look and sound like business leaders. Would you hand that CEO a $3,000,000 check?

Dateline: Houston, TX – XYZ Consultants lost three consecutive proposals. Each debriefing elicited the same response: "Your presentation was flat. You didn't look like you wanted our business." XYZ was stunned. They had devoted significant time and resources to each presentation. XYZ lost the immediate and ongoing revenue from three substantial assignments. They were unaware of how their presentations were being perceived. They had not practiced on videotape to find out just how uninspiring their presentations appeared.

Dateline: Cincinnati, OH – An investment firm loses a large client as a result of a poor presentation. The client later said, "We couldn't believe you were managing our financial future. You couldn't manage a 45-minute presentation."

Dateline: North Carolina – A real estate developer loses a $100 million project because the person leading the proposal completely disengaged from the prospect by reading the entire presentation word for word.

Dateline: Phoenix – An architect loses a $3.5 million job on the basis of what the prospect called a horrible presentation. The poor showing overshadowed an excellent track record.

The architect said he thought the presentation had gone quite well.

What is the cost of average?

In addition to lost revenue and blown opportunities, the cost of average is missing out on the cascade of benefits exceptional presentation skills bring. It is more than you can afford.

Fill out the form on the following page to objectively assess your current skill level.

RATE YOURSELF AS A PRESENTER

Use a scale of 1-10 (10 being best) _____

What are your greatest strengths as a presenter?

_____

_____

An executive once responded: "I really have no strengths, but if I had to list one, I guess it would be humility."

What are your areas of greatest need and refinement?

_____

_____

Are you more comfortable presenting to people you know or people you don't know? _____

What is the difference? _____

Circle one:
Are you a better presenter standing up or sitting down?
Do you prefer: a script, bullet points or off the cuff?

What impression do you make on an audience?

_____

_____

Have you used videotape to critique your effectiveness? _____
If yes, when did you last tape yourself? _____
What did you learn? _____

Rate and evaluate yourself again in 60 days.

CHAPTER FOUR

Organized

Structuring Your Story

The information that follows provides a framework that has proven helpful when preparing clients for presentations, proposals, road shows, interviews, media appearances, question and answer sessions, phone conversations and even important voice mail messages.

This framework will help you alleviate some of your pre-preparation anguish and allow you to efficiently and consistently structure a powerful message.

There are two essential facets of organizing a presentation:

1) Develop a **structure** that allows you to frame your objective, cover all relevant material, transition smoothly from topic to topic and finish strong.

2) **Look organized.** If you don't look organized, the perception will be that you didn't care enough to prepare. You create a negative impression right from the start.

A longstanding presentation structure is:

- Tell them what you're going to tell them (opening).

- Tell them (body).

- Tell them what you just told them (close).

It's a good foundation, and in the following pages we will build on this timeless structure.

Think of a presentation you've recently completed or one that you will soon deliver. Apply the following suggestions to that presentation. Use a proposal, status report, client conversation or keynote speech. This process will be more meaningful if you use material that is "real life."

Presentation to: _____

What did he just say?

Studies suggest that the average adult "undivided attention span" is fifteen to thirty seconds.

Most people will forget 95% of what you say within minutes of hearing your message. That's assuming they hear it in the first place.

- Keep your message compelling.

- Keep your message brief.

- Do everything in your power to keep your audience engaged (see Chapter 6).

- Repeat your key points.

Begin with a Purpose

*"A speech without a purpose is like
a journey without a destination."*
Ralph C. Smedley

Picture yourself in front of your audience. You have come to the end of your presentation. You are determined that they will remember your key points far beyond the end of the meeting. Complete the following sentence.

"If you remember just one thing as you leave here today, remember this:

_____

_____

_____."

By completing that sentence, you have successfully identified the most relevant information in your presentation. As you build the presentation, never lose sight of that one thing. It is your purpose.

Delivering a purpose statement at the beginning of your presentation will keep the audience focused on your key points.

The more defined your purpose, the easier it is to frame your message and stick with it. If you clearly define the purpose of your presentation, you will find it easier to keep your information relevant. You will also avoid delving into areas that are better addressed at a different time and place.

The Four Components of Any Presentation

With a clearly defined purpose, the next step is to develop the four critical components of the presentation:

1. OBJECTIVE / PURPOSE / MISSION / GOAL
Why are we here?

Be prepared to state your objective, mission, goal or purpose. If you cannot clearly define your objective, then there is probably not a compelling reason to do the presentation. The purpose statement and objective set the agenda.

Use phrases such as:

- *"My mission this morning is....,"*
- *"My objective in the next thirty minutes is to....,"*
- *"The purpose of this session is...,"*
- *"I have three goals this afternoon...,"*
- *"If you remember one thing as you leave today's session..."*

By defining the objectives, you signal to your audience that you are organized, prepared and focused. A well-defined objective suggests competence.

2. POSITION / SITUATION / ISSUES
How are things positioned? What is the situation? What are the issues?

Outline the issues, concerns, fears, expectations, successes or obstacles as you understand them.

"As I understand the situation, you are experiencing rising inventories and declining sales. Your receivables are running at fourteen weeks and you recently lost

your biggest customer. You've determined that you don't have the experience or the resources to turn the situation around."

At this point in your presentation stop and ask your audience if anything has changed. Are there other issues that are relevant to the discussion?

"Is there anything else I need to be aware before proceeding?"

"Jill, since we last spoke, have any of your objectives changed?"

I have seen presenters deliver entire proposals without once stopping to make sure that their understanding of the situation was still accurate. Only after the proposal did they find out that a critical piece of information had changed and their solutions were no longer relevant. The earlier you ask about changes, the easier it is to adjust your presentation accordingly.

3. END RESULT / BENEFITS / CONSEQUENCES
What are the benefits, ramifications, consequences and implications of taking or not taking action?

"As a result of our falling sales, we've lost 7% market share in the last 12 months."

"The implication of our increased inventory is that we will be forced to shut down the Jacksonville plant for thirty days."

"Our focus on efficiency in the last two quarters has resulted in an additional $22 million to our bottom line."

"The benefit of acting on the proposal today will be seen in the form of additional revenue in the next 90 days."

4. NEXT STEP / ACTION PLAN / TIME LINE
What is the next step? What are the expectations? Where do we go from here?

Use the next step as your call to action. It will help prepare your audience for what you expect of them and what they can expect of you. The next step can be as simple as, "Let's meet again on Wednesday." Or it can set the stage for significant and detailed follow up.

"Our next step is to ramp up marketing efforts in the East."

"Our plan is to launch the new program by April 1st."

"Going forward, I would like you to meet with your team and select a leader to manage the project."

"We need to finalize the contract by Friday."

How to "Tell Them What You're Going to Tell Them"

Example: 60-second opening using all four components

*My **objective** this afternoon is to persuade you to approve the purchase of the ZXC inventory software in order to put an end to our inventory crisis.*

*Our current **position** is one of reacting to inventory changes instead of anticipating customer demand. We recently lost two significant customers because of botched orders. We have an additional problem in that our regional offices are unable to communicate inventory fluctuations to a central location.*

*The **end result** of our inventory inefficiency is that we're losing customers and we're losing $3 million per quarter.*

If we upgrade to the ZXC software, we will benefit by holding onto the $3 million per quarter, and our more efficient response time will create greater customer loyalty.

*The **next step** is to approve the purchase of the software this afternoon and have it in place within 30 days.*

The objective of the meeting is clear. There's no confusion as to how the company is positioned. The cost of inaction and the benefits of taking action are stated up front. Participants understand what the presenter is recommending.

There are other approaches to creating a powerful objective statement. Let's change the order of the components and note the effect.

*The **situation** is as follows. We are using antiquated inventory software. Our response time to customer requests is unacceptable. In addition, our regional offices have no way of communicating inventory status to a central location.*

*The **end result** of our inefficiency is that we're losing $3 million per quarter and we're losing customers.*

*My **objective** this afternoon is to persuade you to purchase new inventory software immediately in order to correct this situation.*

*The **next step** is for us to approve the purchase of the new ZXC inventory software and have it in place within 30 days.*

You may have noticed that this arrangement of the four components draws more attention to the objective.

Each opening took less than forty-five seconds to deliver.

Frame Your "Real Life" Presentation

Craft a sixty-second opening consisting your purpose statement and the four components. Use them in any order. Time your completed opening.

Begin each segment with the following words:

If you remember one thing from our session today, remember this:

_____

_____

My objective (purpose, mission, goal) today is

_____

_____

We are currently positioned OR The situation is as follows

_____

_____

The end result (benefit, consequence, ramification)

_____

_____

Our next step

_____

_____

You have just defined your opening and framed your entire presentation.

How to "Tell Them"

Use the same framework for the body of your presentation. You can go into greater detail in the body of the presentation. How much time you spend in each segment depends on what you are attempting to accomplish.

Use stories, examples and anecdotes to help fix your message in the minds of your audience. Keep every piece of information relevant. Stay focused on what you want them to remember.

Be sure to work on your transitions from segment to segment. If your information flows smoothly, you will appear more knowledgeable than a presenter who fumbles from one topic to the next.

"Now that we've discussed the benefits of the new system, let's lay out the steps and the timing of implementation."

How to "Tell Them What You Just Told Them"

Summarize what you have presented to them.

"In summary, our target clients need to fall into one of two categories:

> *#1 ....*
>
> *#2 ....*

If we stay true to this plan, we will have more qualified prospects and our win ratio should jump dramatically."

End with a Purpose Statement

What you say last will be remembered most. We started our presentation framework by establishing a purpose. A purpose statement is an effective way to end your presentation.

The purpose statement provides the one, two or three key points your audience must remember as they leave the room. The shorter and more direct the purpose statement, the greater its impact.

Question and answer sessions can occur during or after your presentation. If you open the floor to questions after your presentation, be sure to end the session by drawing the attention of your audience back to your purpose.

The quality of the questions oftentimes diminishes as Q&A proceeds. Don't end your session on a low note. Don't end your presentation with the final question. Use your purpose statement to hammer home your key points one final time. Make sure your audience remembers the strongest points of your session. You don't want an irrelevant answer to an irrelevant question ringing in their ears as they leave.

Wrap up the Q&A and close your session by delivering your "purpose statement."

"If there are no further questions, keep in mind that we owe our existence to our customers. Do everything humanly possible to service their every need."

"If there are no further questions, keep in mind that the destiny of this organization is not a matter of chance, it is a matter of choice. The choices we make in the next 30 days will decide our fate."

At the end of this chapter and in the back of this book are prep sheets that will help you prepare for your next presentation.

Attention-Grabbing Openings

Beginning the presentation with a purpose or objective is both effective and functional. However, exceptional presenters go a step further: they add an attention-grabbing opener. An ineffective opening can handicap your entire presentation. Set the expectations within 60-90 seconds that your message is worth their undivided attention.

Use the first sixty seconds to lay the foundation. This is not the time to go into extensive detail. Use the body of the presentation to delve into as much detail as you need, or as much as time constraints dictate.

If you want to start your presentation with something other than the objective, you have many options from which to choose.

As you become more proficient at structuring your message, you can try more creative and more flexible ways to start your presentation.

- **A quote:**

  "When one door of opportunity closes, another opens; but often we look so long at the closed door that we do not see the one which has been opened for us." Helen Keller

- **A statistic:**

  "The next time you deliver a speech, keep in mind that 90% of what you're about to say will be forgotten within 60 minutes."

- **A question to the audience:**

  "What is the greatest challenge facing your business today?"

- **A current news item or periodical:**

  "According to today's Wall Street Journal ..."

- **A story that relates directly to your message:**

  Suppose you are speaking on the topic of leadership: *"Willie Shoemaker, one of horse racing's greatest jockeys, said, 'I always tried to keep the lightest possible grip on the horse's reins. The horse never knows I'm there until he needs me.'"*

- **A sincere thank you or acknowledgment:**

  "I'd like to thank the Academy for this honor."

- **Have them write something down:**

  "There are six characteristics shared by the world's most exceptional speakers. You probably want to write these down."

- **Humor:**

  President George W. Bush would often begin his campaign stump speeches by saying, *"Before I left Texas my wife Laura said to me, 'honey don't try to be charming, don't try to be witty, don't try to be eloquent, just be yourself.'"*

- **Make a prediction:**

  "By the time you leave here today, I predict that you will have a plan in place to increase your sales by 15% to 20%."

- **A poem or rhyme:**

  "Give me your tired, your poor, Your huddled masses yearning to breathe free, The wretched refuse of your teeming shore. Send these, the homeless, tempest-tost to me. I lift my lamp beside the golden door!" A poem by Emma Lazarus that is graven on a tablet within the pedestal of the Statue of Liberty.

- **An extended pause**

If You Don't Look Organized, You Won't Appear Prepared

We've all seen a presenter begin his speech by looking down, shuffling notes, hemming and hawing, clearing his throat, testing the microphone and tucking in his shirt. The presenter has had several weeks to prepare; yet he appears completely caught off guard by the fact that it's his turn to speak.

Even if this presenter is a leading authority on the topic, his thirty seconds of floundering sends the opposite signal to his audience. As management guru Tom Peters says, "Perception is reality." The audience sees a presenter who is not prepared. His perceived lack of preparation is interpreted as a lack of respect for his audience. It also creates questions as to his level of confidence in what he is about to present.

We have one chance to make a first impression. Or, as a client in Texas put it, "You have one chance to kiss the pig." Don't fritter away that one chance by appearing unprepared.

We begin judging people the instant we make visual contact. Audiences will judge you before you utter your first word. Do you look prepared?

Stand

Set your notes

Establish eye contact

Pause for 3-4 seconds

Smile

State your purpose

The 60/20 Rule

Arrive 60 minutes before you are scheduled to present. Use the first 40 minutes to prepare: the room, seating, notes, AV equipment, handouts and props.

The 20 minutes prior to your presentation is prime time for introductions, information gathering and rapport building.

This is not the time for rearranging chairs, dragging tables across the floor, pounding your keyboard to get the computer working, fiddling with your projector, collating handouts or frantically shuffling through your notes in a last-ditch effort to rehearse.

Own the Room! You are responsible for the success or failure of the session. When the audience arrives, turn your undivided attention to meeting and greeting. Introduce audience members to one another. Be a conversation starter.

You can gather a great deal of valuable and relevant information in 20 minutes. Incorporate this information into your presentation. "Karen, you mentioned prior to our session that you recently had an wonderful customer service experience. Could you share it with everyone?" Karen feels good because you remembered her name, you involved her in the presentation, and she had the opportunity to contribute to the session.

Following the 60/20 Rule will help you appear more prepared. It will also eliminate last minute changes that can cause last minute panic.

PRESENTATION PREP SHEET

Presentation to: _____

Date: _____ **Time:** _____

What is the most important thing for your audience to remember?

_____

_____

STRUCTURING YOUR PRESENTATION

My objective (Mission, Purpose, Goal) is:

_____

_____

We are positioned as follows or the situation is as follows:

_____

_____

* * Ask if your understanding of the situation is correct.

The end result (Benefits, Consequences):

_____

_____

Next step:

_____

_____

Close with your Purpose Statement — "As you leave, I would like you to remember…"

_____

_____

OUTLINE

Opening – Objective: _____

_____

Body of Presentation

    Point #1:
    Support:

    Point #2:
    Support:

    Point #3:
    Support:

Summary: _____

_____

Purpose Statement: _____

_____

HELPFUL INFO TO REVIEW

Who will lead the presentation? _____

What are the roles of team members? _____

Who will attend? _____

A/V requirements: _____

Handouts: _____

Stories/Anecdotes: _____

Contact name and number: _____

CHAPTER FIVE

Passionate

*"The orator is the embodiment of the passions
of the multitude. Before he can inspire them with
any emotion he must be swayed by it himself.
Before he can move their tears his own must flow.
To convince them he must himself believe."*
Sir Winston Churchill

Exceptional presenters radiate passion, conviction and enthusiasm. I frequently survey business professionals and ask them to list the characteristics of exceptional presenters. Passionate is the #1 response.

If you don't look and sound passionate about your topic, why would your audience be passionate about your topic?

Feeling passionate is one thing. Looking and sounding passionate is quite another. Our body language, facial expressions, movement, gestures and voice are the implements that convert words into action and transform the printed text into emotion and enthusiasm.

Passionate presenters are more persuasive.

If you want your audience to take action, it is not enough to convince them of your position. They can be convinced, but continue to do nothing. It's more important to persuade them to take action.

Passion is expressed almost entirely through delivery. We can take a passionate, heartfelt, moving speech and turn it into a sleeper by delivering that speech in a monotone, uninspired fashion.

Take the speech by Martin Luther King, Jr., delivered on the steps of the Lincoln Memorial on August 23, 1963. He spoke to over a quarter of a million people. The spirit of his "I have a dream" speech and the words he spoke still resonate in the hearts and minds of Americans everywhere. His speech was passion personified.

Imagine taking King's script and asking Henry Kissinger to deliver the speech. The impact would be quite different.

There is no one style for passion. It shows up in different delivery styles. Oprah Winfrey demonstrates open, engaging passion. Colin Powell exudes an intense, straightforward passion. Regis Philbin unleashes an exuberant and spirited passion.

Because passion is expressed through our delivery, we will focus our attention on the following skill sets:

- Posture
- Gestures and movement
- Voice command
- Eliminating hesitation and verbal graffiti

"Nothing great can be achieved
without enthusiasm."
Ralph Waldo Emerson

The Power of Non-verbal Communication

Your non-verbal messages will override anything you say. If you say, "I'm confident that we'll complete the project on time and on budget," but you are backpedaling and looking at your shoes when you say it, the audience will believe your body language. Your words are undermined by your retreating body language. Your words and your non-verbal messages must be congruent.

Posture

What role does body language play in our ability to communicate passionately? Dr. Mehrabian's study revealed that **55%** of our impact is determined by our non-verbal messages (body language, movement, eye contact, appearance, facial expressions and gestures).

People begin judging us as soon as they establish visual contact. What do they see that enables them to judge us so quickly? Their judgements are based, to a great extent, on how we carry ourselves.

How do you carry yourself? Do you stand straight, or do you slouch? Do you exude confidence, or do you exude apathy? Do you move with purpose, or do you drag yourself from place to place?

Posture and carriage are excellent indicators of one's confidence, comfort level, experience and attitude. In many cases, posture is our first line of communication.

> **Situation** – You're attending a networking function. You glance at the door as person A enters the room. You know nothing about this person, but your immediate evaluation is that she is confident, professional and credible. You sense that this would be a good person to meet. She has an aura about her.

What visual clues led to those conclusions?

_____

_____

_____

_____

Here are some of the clues you might have picked up on:

- She stood tall and attentive.
- She moved with purpose, keeping her head and eyes up.
- She appeared comfortable making eye contact, even if she didn't know the other person.
- She smiled easily and was quick to offer a handshake.
- You could almost see her energy being transferred to others, and her openness revealed her enthusiasm for the event.

At the same function you see person B. It's easy to see that he had absolutely no interest in attending the function. You sensed that he also had no interest in the people attending the function.

What visual clues led to your conclusions about person B?

_____

_____

_____

_____

Here are some of the clues you might have picked up on:

- He slouched.
- His head and eyes remained down for the most part.
- He would look up long enough to find a familiar face. If he didn't spot a familiar face, his eyes would dart back to the floor.

- His face was expressionless.

- He glanced at his watch several times.

- He labored from one spot to the next.

- He offered no handshakes or greetings.

- His first stop was to the cash bar for a shot of liquid personality.

If Dr. Mahrabian's study is accurate and 55% of our communication is non-verbal, then we will be able to make a positive first impression every time. We simply need to be aware of the messages we're sending and adjust our non-verbals accordingly.

As presenters we begin making impressions before we open our mouths to speak. Before we utter our first word, our presence has spoken volumes. We expose our personalities in the way we carry ourselves, in our attire and outward attitude.

What Is the Most Effective Standing Position?

Exercise:

When you are in a position to move about safely, stand up and stretch your arms to the side. Stretch your arms up. Reach for the sky. Now, for 30 seconds, close your eyes and completely relax your arms, shoulders, hands and forearms. Relax your head and neck.

When you were completely relaxed, where were your hands? Chances are, your hands were at your sides.

When I conduct this exercise at the beginning of seminars, 99% of the people in the room assume the "relaxed" position, their hands and arms resting at their sides.

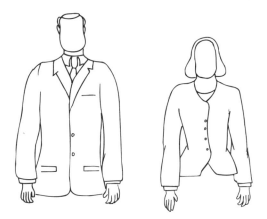

"Hands at the sides" is an excellent base position. Remaining in that position for extended periods would cause a person to look stiff. But as a base position, between gestures and movements, it creates a strong, relaxed presence and helps eliminate distractions.

With your hands at your sides, you appear open, eager, confident and seasoned. You do not appear defensive or like you are trying to hide something.

Occasionally, police officers will attend my workshops. Some have told me that they are trained to approach potentially confrontational situations with their hands at their sides. They want to appear in complete command of the situation. They can't afford to appear hesitant, diffident or threatening.

Exercise:

Suppose your team is running behind schedule on a key project. You deliver the following statement to them. "Ladies and gentlemen, we <u>must</u> work together and we <u>must</u> find the solution quickly. Otherwise we will lose this customer. (Dramatic pause) Losing this customer is not an option." Circle the posture that would create the maximum impact for your message to your team. X out the posture that would create the least impact.

Standing with your hands at your sides takes no effort. You are built to stand that way. Your wrists, arms and shoulder muscles are relaxed. You look relaxed even when you are nervous.

When you are not using your hands to gesture, keep them at your sides.

The Most Common Presentation Posture

T-Rex

The most common posture presenters assume is what I call the T-Rex position. Picture a Tyrannosaurus Rex with those tiny arms dangling in front of its massive body. The arms don't appear to have a purpose. They just hang there.

Presenters frequently assume the T-Rex position. The hands just dangle in front of the body. I'm sure you've seen it many times. The presenter's arms are locked. As the mouth moves, so do the hands. The hands flail in a futile attempt to participate. The hands appear completely out-of-sync with the message. At times, the hands and mouth appear to be delivering different speeches.

If you are in a position to do so safely, assume the T-Rex position. Standing or sitting, it doesn't matter. Join me and engage in some of the distracting activities that occur as a result of T-Rex. See how these feel. You have probably already engaged in several of these activities:

- The "spider on the mirror." Fingertips touching fingertips.

- The "sisters of mercy." Hands in the praying position.

- The "fire starter." Rubbing the hands together in a furious attempt to ignite the brain.

- The "ring leader." Twirling, twisting and tugging the ring.

- The "hand washer." Scrub up.

- "The cuff tugger." Can't get those cuffs out far enough.

Locked in the T-Rex position, presenters unknowingly perform world class baton twirling routines with pens. They click dry erase markers repeatedly, without a clue that each click sounds to the audience like a shotgun blast. They leaf through notes and turn paper into telescopes. They straighten and reshape paper clips. They check the position of their tie, multiple times. They even clean their fingernails.

By avoiding the T-Rex position you will immediately eliminate numerous distracting idiosyncrasies.

Other Speaker Positions and the Messages They Send:

FIG LEAF	HANDS IN POCKETS	PARADE REST
Timid, pensive, inexperienced, feeling vulnerable	Nonchalant, passive, over-confident	Sheepish, withholding info, hiding something

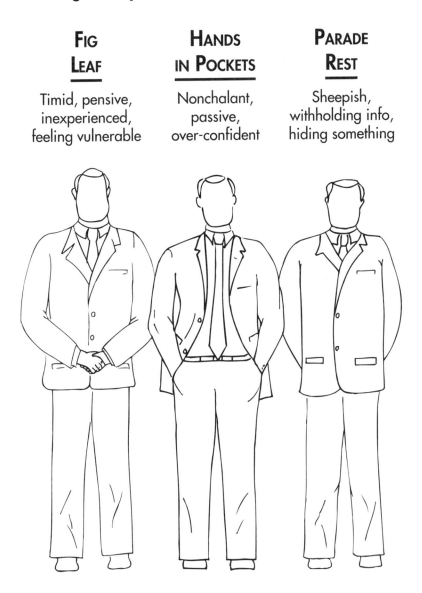

HANDS ON HIPS

Challenging,
defiant, overbearing

"You gotta problem with that?"
"We'd better buckle down."

ARMS CROSSED

Closed off,
restrained

"I'm not buying what
you're saying."

What Is the Most Effective Seated Position?

People tend to get lazy or lax at meetings in which everyone is seated. Be comfortable, but don't be lazy. Don't slouch in your chair. Don't rest your head in your hands.

Keep your hands on the table.

Ann Marie Sabath, a leading expert on business etiquette, recommends that when we are dining out with clients, we should keep our hands on the table. She suggests that, with our hands on the table, we look engaged in the discussion and more interested in what others have to say.

Ann Marie's advice about using your hands at dinner also applies to presenting at a table or a desk. We should keep our hands on the table. We appear more interested and attentive. We can use our hands freely to gesture. Leaning toward the table adds energy to our delivery. Sit with your back straight without being rigid. You will appear to have greater enthusiasm for your topic.

Most of your forearms should be on the table. Just like mom always told you, "Keep your elbows off the dinner table." The same goes for presentations.

When seated, keep your hands at least eight to ten inches into the table when gesturing. Hands on the edge of the table look like puppets. It also makes you look tentative.

Square Up

An excellent way to personalize your message is to square your shoulders to the person with whom you are making eye contact. Most presenters only move their head from side to side when making eye contact. Squaring your shoulders invites each person into the presentation.

Squaring up also helps to stabilize your feet and keeps you from drifting, shuffling and swaying.

If you are presenting to a large audience, square up to people in different parts of the room. Remember to square up to the people all the way to your right and left. Draw them into your presentation. You should also do this when presenting from behind a lectern.

It is difficult to ignore someone who is squared up to you and looking you directly in the eye. It feels personal and conversational.

When seated at a conference table, you can still square your shoulders to various audience members. Don't swivel your chair each time you redirect your eye contact to someone new. Rather, during your presentation, randomly square up and establish eye contact.

Presenting From Behind a Lectern

Here are a few techniques to use when presenting from behind a lectern.

Anything you stand behind during a presentation can act as a barrier between you and your audience. If forced to speak from a lectern, make a special effort to connect.

- Make eye contact with all parts of the room.

  There is a tendency to focus on the people immediately in front of you. Square your shoulders to the people all the way to your right and to your left. Draw them in. You can accomplish this even when using a microphone.

- Keep your head and eyes up.

  If you stand with your stomach pressed against the lectern and your notes are resting on the ledge of the lectern, then the audience will completely lose sight of your face every time you glance at your notes.

  Slide your notes toward the front of the lectern. Depending on the incline of the lectern, you might need to hold them in place with one hand. Move three to four inches away from the lectern. Now you are in a position to glance at your notes without moving your head. Only your eyes move. People in the back of the room will not even realize that you are using notes.

- Use your hands freely to gesture.

- Notes on loose-leaf paper tend to fall off lecterns. Practice using various note holders to determine what works best for you (5x7 index cards, a three-ring binder, a flip pad...).

Fidgety Hands

Fidgety hands tend to make us appear uncomfortable. In his book, *Telling Lies,* author Paul Ekman writes that his research shows that fidgety hands often reflect a level of discomfort. The perception of someone viewing a fidgety communicator is that the communicator is nervous, uncomfortable with the topic or distorting or avoiding the truth. The more manipulators (rubbing, scratching, touching, or fidgeting) a viewer sees, according to Ekman, the less the viewer tends to trust the information coming from the person using the manipulators.

If you want to build greater credibility with your audience, eliminate fidgety movements and nervous looking activity.

Can You Handle the PRESSURE?

Under pressure, our bodies seek to be comfortable. We can physically retreat without even realizing it.

- Head and eyes lowering
- Hands diving into the pockets
- Clasping hands behind the back
- Eyes darting to the ceiling or floor
- Backpedaling
- Grappling hands
- Fidgeting with pens, markers or notes
- Hemming and hawing
- Grabbing the back of a chair for support
- Fingers dancing on the table
- Using verbal graffiti, such as um and uh

FIVE TIPS TO APPEAR
RELAXED, CONFIDENT AND PROFESSIONAL

1) Stand tall — don't sway, rock, shuffle or lean.

2) Keep your head and eyes up. Connect with your audience.

3) Smile. A sincere smile warms up the coldest situations.

4) Never retreat.

5) Move with purpose, energy and enthusiasm.

Practicing to Solidify Exceptional Posture

For the next 30 days:

- Practice every time you stand up. Put your hands at your sides.

- Practice the hands down position in every conversation.

- Practice whenever you are standing in line.

- Practice by noticing where others place their hands, especially when under pressure.

- If you have a habit of fidgeting with your hands, keep your hands apart even when you are sitting down. Fidgeting with your hands while seated reinforces a bad habit and makes it more difficult to relax the hands when you are standing.

If you practice your posture for the next 30 days, the hands down position should become your most comfortable position. You should prefer the hands down position to all others (fig leaf, hands in pockets, parade rest, hands on hips or T-Rex).

Gestures

A study by Jana Iverson, University of Missouri Psychologist, concluded that moving our hands when we speak is innate. She said, *"We're born with a propensity to move our hands when we speak."*

Iverson's study included the use of gestures by blind children. Blind children will routinely gesture when describing objects, even when they're describing the objects to other blind children. Her conclusion was that gestures are very closely linked to the way we communicate and express ourselves.

Another study conducted at the Columbia University revealed that gestures are our way of expressing ourselves and being understood. We use gestures as cues to trigger our recollection.

If you are going to use your hands to gesture, be specific.

There is a tendency for presenters to do one of two things with their hands: 1) restrict their movement in an attempt not to flail, or 2) flail.

Conduct your own study:

- Notice how your hands move when you're talking with close friends or family members.

- Notice your hands when you're giving someone driving directions.

- Notice your hands when you're determined to move someone to your point of view.

- Notice how defined your movements become when you are in a heated argument.

- Notice how other people use their hands while speaking.

- Notice your hands while you are talking on the telephone. It's no wonder some states have outlawed the use of cell phones while driving. The driver is talking and gesturing wildly with both hands, leaving only the knees to steer the vehicle.

What you will notice is that you use your hands quite freely and expressively. It is hard to restrict the use of our hands when we are excited, angry, adamant or determined. Typically, the more animated we become, the more specific and defined our gestures become.

A University of Texas study found that people remember more of what they see than what they hear. Think of your gestures as traveling visual aids.

Use gestures to bring an additional visual dimension to your presentation. Gestures will boost the amount of information your audience retains.

Almost anything you can design in a computer-generated visual, you can describe using gestures.

Five Effective Ways to Incorporate Gestures

1. WHEN USING "THE CLAW," YOUR MOST VERSATILE GESTURE

The "claw" can and should be used often. It reflects an image of a seasoned professional. It can be used standing or seated, behind a lectern or behind a desk.

At the flip chart, dry erase board and screen it enables a presenter to maintain eye contact with and keep her shoulders square to the entire audience.

Watch *The Weather Channel*. The meteorologists do an excellent job of using the claw at the screen while keeping their shoulders square to the camera.

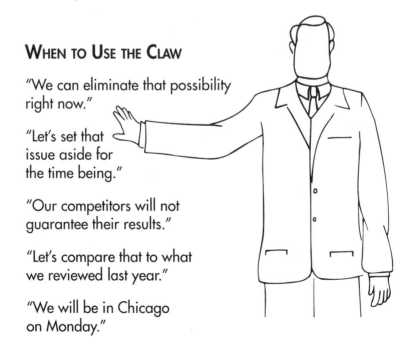

WHEN TO USE THE CLAW

"We can eliminate that possibility right now."

"Let's set that issue aside for the time being."

"Our competitors will not guarantee their results."

"Let's compare that to what we reviewed last year."

"We will be in Chicago on Monday."

2. WHEN USING NUMBERS

Use the numbers one through five. Stop at five.

"If you remember only one thing this afternoon..."

"The two primary concerns I have are..."

"We have three objectives this afternoon."

"The client wants this competed in four days."

"There are five reasons this election is critical."

3. WHEN USING COMPARISONS

"Revenue increased from $300 million last year to $420 million this year."

"Profits have decreased from 13% to 7%."

"Headcount has increased from 35 employees to 47 employees."

"The lead has grown from 4% to 7% since the debate."

4. WHEN USING VERBS

"Our goal is to **increase** revenue while we **decrease** our inventory." (See sketch on page 69.)

"We will **expand** our existing product line."

"Let's **eliminate** that possibility right now."

5. WHEN PINPOINTING DATES AND WHEN USING TIMELINES

"The start date is June 6th."

"We will offer the incentives until July 15th."

"Between now and August 15th, this is our top priority."

Practice Opportunities Abound

Well-defined gestures must become second nature or they can appear ill timed and forced.

- Use crisp, specific gestures in every conversation.

- Practice while you are on the phone. The more defined your movements, the stronger and more direct your voice will sound.

- Volunteer to give directions to anyone who looks lost.

- Purchase an American Sign Language dictionary. Many of the signs are common gestures.

- If asked how many sugars you want in your coffee, don't just tell them "two." Tell them and show them.

- If someone comments on your beautiful wall paper, give them a step-by-step, gesture filled review of how you measured the area, cut the paper, dunked it in the water, unraveled it and carefully matched up the strips. (You are probably visualizing someone wallpapering as you read this.)

Gestures become second nature through repetition. You cannot become proficient using them only once in a while. The more you gesture in casual conversations, the less you'll have to think about them when you're presenting.

Do not think about your gestures during your presentation. It will only serve to throw you off track. Limit your gestures when reading a scripted presentation. It looks forced.

Gestures in Summary

- NO T-REX. Get your elbows away from your ribcage.

- Use your hands freely.

- Think of gestures as your permanent visual aids.

- Be specific, be specific, be specific. The more defined you look, the more defined your message appears to your audience.

- Don't rush. Fast gestures are ineffective. They resemble flailing hands. Hold your gestures for 2-4 seconds.

- After gesturing, place your hands back at your sides.

- Use both hands. There is a tendency for right handers to make all right handed gestures. Left handers, same thing. Continually using the same hand looks repetitive.

- Avoid the bungie effect where it looks like your hands are tied together with a bungie cord. Where one hand goes, the other follows. Use one-handed gestures in addition to two-handed gestures. One-handed gestures get your point across with less movement.

- Don't make your gestures the focal point of your presentation. Use gestures to assist your audience in understanding your message.

The Dynamics of Voice

If you don't sound interested, why should I be interested?

Use arrows to match the names with the voice description.
Names can have more than one description.

Passionate	Ronald Reagan	Monotone
Dynamic	Bill Clinton	Stiff / scripted
	Barbara Walters	
Inspirational	Oprah Winfrey	Dry
Enthusiastic	John F. Kennedy	Boring
Commanding	Martin Luther King	Flat
	Colin Powell	
Conversational	Katie Couric	Weak
Lively	Rosie O'Donnell	Uninspired
Fun	Jesse Jackson	Sing-songy
	Dick Vitale	
Friendly	Elizabeth Dole	Dull
Interesting	Tom Brokaw	Inaudible
Spellbinding	Norman Schwarzkopf	Lazy
	Jane Pauley	
Appealing	Paul Harvey	Irritating
Intense	Regis Philbin	Tired
Calming	Billy Graham	Listless
	Your voice?	

Did your arrows tend to point in the same direction?
Who do you know who fits the descriptions on the right?

Your voice is an outward expression of your passion. Your voice can add energy, animation and excitement to your presentation.

Volume

People associate a strong voice with confidence.
People associate a weak voice with a lack of confidence.

Develop a strong, confident voice.
Don't scream. Don't yell. Just SPEAK UP.

Most people do not come close to tapping the full potential of their voice. The voice is a valuable tool to becoming an exceptional presenter.

Very few people have audio taped or videotaped themselves delivering a presentation. As a result, they have no way of knowing how their voices sound. The only way to improve the quality of your voice is to know what others are hearing when you speak.

When we get nervous, we tend to speed up our delivery. The more we speed up, the less we breathe. We find ourselves speaking from the throat, instead of allowing our diaphragm and lungs to help boost our decibel level. Speaking from the top of the throat results in a thinner, softer voice.

It can be difficult for soft-spoken people to elevate their volume to an effective level. If one's voice is soft, doubling the volume is barely noticeable to the listeners, but it sounds like shouting to the speaker. People should not have to strain to hear your message. If you speak after taking a breath, you will create more volume and resonance with less effort.

Inflection

According to Dr. Merhabian's studies, 84% of the impact you have over the phone comes from your voice whereas 16% of your impact comes from the words you use.

Call a friend at work. You can guess her mood by the tone in her voice when she answers the phone. You can hear her attitude.

Expand the range of your voice. A monotone voice will significantly shorten the attention span of your audience.

Pacing/Tempo

When we get nervous, we tend to speed up.

When we speed up, we forget to breathe. If we're not breathing, we're not pausing. Words tend to run together. Soon, everything sounds the same.

SPEAK, PAUSE, BREATHE, SPEAK

Listen to exceptional communicators. They take their time. They articulate their thoughts. They don't rush. By pausing and breathing, they are able to make words, phrases, numbers and statistics stand out.

People do not hang on every word we say. That is why we need to be deliberate. Use pace and inflection to make your words jump out at your audience. Force the listener to hear what is important for them to hear.

Practice Tapping Your Full Voice Potential

Once you expand the range of your voice, monotone will no longer be acceptable. Your voice will only improve with practice. There are many opportunities during your daily routines to practice the volume, inflection and pace of your vocal delivery.

- Practice every time you leave a voice mail message. Check each message before sending it.

- Practice by reading out loud. Read your favorite morning periodical out loud at the breakfast table. Or close your office door and read aloud as if your voice was being broadcast to listeners all around the country.

- Read children's books to your kids. Use different voices to represent the various characters.

- Mimic radio commercials and disk jockeys. Radio commercials are fast and at the high end of the energy level. They are good for stretching your comfort level. The goal is not to have everyone sound like Dick Vitale or Richard Simmons. The goal is to encourage you to use your full voice potential.

- Read billboards out loud.

- Notice your voice when you are having a lively conversation with friends or family members. Is it more animated than your presentation voice? It shouldn't be.

- Mimic the voices of politicians and celebrities. Try these: Bill Clinton, George W. Bush, Barbara Walters, Donald Trump, Diane Sawyer, and Jay Leno.

Your voice should bring energy, excitement and enthusiasm to your presentation.

Don't be monotone.

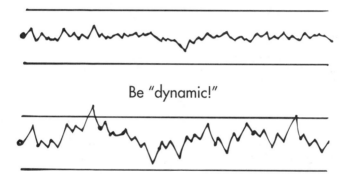

Be "dynamic!"

Eliminate Verbal Graffiti

Call it verbal graffiti, call it trash, call it filler, call it padding. Call it anything you want, but be sure to call it "unprofessional." Most importantly, eliminate it from your vocabulary.

Clearly, filler *um* adds *like* nothing to our effectiveness, *you know what I mean? Um, basically* it *like* dilutes the impact of our *um* message, *OK? And, to be honest with you* (I've been lying to you up until now), it causes us, *you know,* to sound *um* unprepared and *um* unprofessional, *see?*

Some will argue that filler is conversational. They contend that filler is natural and does not impact the message. I vehemently disagree.

Has the President of the United States <u>ever</u> written filler into a State of the Union address or Inaugural speech? The answer is no. If filler was natural and conversational, you would think the President would direct his speechwriters to "Throw in a dozen or so ums and six or seven you knows."

Martin Luther King did not use filler in his impassioned "I have a dream" speech. It wasn't the "I have a um, you know, like a dream" speech.

In an Inaugural speech that inspired mankind to put a man on the moon, John F. Kennedy did not say, "To be honest with you, fellow Americans, we um basically choose to, you know, put a man on the uh moon."

The filler phrase I get the biggest kick out of is, "To be honest with you." Have you been lying to me up until now? Three minutes later the person will say, "To be perfectly honest with you." I see, you were being honest before, now you're really going to be honest.

Television sit-com characters rarely use filler unless the character is supposed to appear uninformed, uneducated or confused.

Practice Techniques for Eliminating Filler

Practice every day until filler is no longer a part of your working vocabulary. From this point forward:

- Do not use filler while leaving voice mail messages. Listen to your outgoing voice mail before hitting the send button.

- Notice how much filler other people use in voice mail messages. Does it sound professional?

- Eliminate filler in casual conversations.

- Record yourself during phone conversations (you don't need to record both sides of the conversation). Listen to the tape for filler. Try to determine your filler patterns.

You will soon be able to anticipate your filler. If you can anticipate it, you can eliminate it.

Filler can become ingrained in your vocabulary. It will most likely take two to four months to eliminate your existing filler. How long it takes will depend entirely on your determination. If you want it out, you can get it out.

Other commonly used graffiti, filler and non-words:

We **clearly** must move on this. It is **clearly**....

We **actually** have a process and it **actually** works.

Frankly I'm not concerned. I **frankly** think we should...

We will proceed cautiously, **and so on and so forth**.

To be honest, I don't know.

Well, there you go again.

Like I said before, we're working on it.

I mean, they took the contract and, **I mean**, tore it up.

Qualifiers

Words that dilute your impact and sound timid.

I think we need to move on this.	vs	We need to move on this.
I guess it's time to begin.	vs	It's time to begin.
We **kinda** missed the deadline.	vs	We missed the deadline.
I **sorta** secured the account.	vs	I secured the account.
Maybe we should reduce inventory.	vs	We should reduce inventory.

There are times when "I think" and "I guess" are appropriate. Use them sparingly.

Be Aware of the "Condescendors"

What are they? They are words we add on at the end of statements. We use them to make sure the audience is with us. Used too often, they sound condescending.

You need to sign this by next week, **OK?**
After it's signed, return it to us, **OK?**
If it's approved, we'll move forward, **OK?**

Repeat the sentences replacing **OK** with "**see.**"
Repeat the sentences replacing **see** with "**right.**"

Condescendors leave the impression that the presenter is not confident in the listener's ability to comprehend the information.

What verbal graffiti do you use?

_____

_____

_____

What verbal graffiti do you notice other people using?

_____

_____

_____

How Do I Eliminate Filler From My Vocabulary?

The use of filler is a habit, just as body language is a habit. How do you change the habit of using verbal graffiti?

Step one to eliminating verbal graffiti and non-words: Recognize the filler you tend to use and listen for the patterns in which you use it. Many people use "um" to start sentences instead of starting with the first word of the sentence.

Step two to eliminating verbal graffiti and non-words: Silence. Use a pause instead of using the filler.

Now that we've covered the majority of the delivery techniques, use the following observation sheet to analyze a TV guest.

Note: There are additional observation sheets in the back of the book. It is recommended that you fill one out for the next three weeks to reinforce what you've learned.

OBSERVATION SHEET

We learn a great deal from observing others. Analyze guests being interviewed on TV shows such as, *Meet the Press, This Week, Hardball, 20/20, O'Reilly Factor, Crossfire* and *60 Minutes*.

Show: _____   Date: _____

Guest: _____   Host: _____

Initial impression of guest: _____

Message was: Well defined / diluted / sidetracked

Why: _____

Write the first two words or sounds of the guest's answers:

_____   _____   _____

Physical presence
Fidgety? If so, how? _____

Were movements and gestures: Defined / limited / nebulous

Adjustments in chair: Frequent / noticeable / infrequent

Posture: Strong / passive / weak. Describe: _____

Eye contact: Sustained / fleeting.

Voice: Unwavering / cautious / hesitant

Filler used and frequency: _____

Did content dictate comfort level? _____

If so, how? _____

Rate the effectiveness of the guest (1 being disastrous and 10 being successful): _____

Overall observations: _____

Chapter Six

Engaging

To earn their respect,
you must first connect

Exceptional presenters connect with their audience. They build rapport quickly and involve the audience early and often.

If you fail to show a genuine interest in your audience, why should they be interested in you or your message?

Five surefire ways to alienate yourself from any audience:

1) Talk about yourself.
2) Avoid eye contact.
3) Don't smile.
4) Read your entire speech.
5) Use inappropriate or sarcastic humor.

An engaging presenter has the ability to draw the audience in and create a conversational atmosphere. Engaging presenters sound as though they are having a lively conversation with friends instead of sounding scripted, didactic or speechy.

Rules of Engagement

Here are 11 ways exceptional presenters connect with their audiences:

1. SPEAK TO THE INTERESTS OF YOUR AUDIENCE

As the saying goes, "People don't care how much you know, until they know how much you care."

Presenters often make the mistake of talking about what is important to them, not to the audience. Your audience couldn't care less about what's important to you. Engage your audience by talking about what's important to them.

How do you know what is important to your audience? You ask. See Chapter Eight, "Understand Your Audience."

It amazes me how many proposals end up being a Niagra Falls of information about the presenter or her company. It's the classic, "Hey, we've been talking about me for the last twenty minutes. What about you? What do you think of me?"

- **"I've been in business for 22 years?"**
  Congratulations, but does that mean I should do business with your competitor because they've been in business 25 years?

- **"We have 350 locations worldwide?"**
  Big deal. What does that mean to my business in South Bend, Indiana? How are your other 349 locations going to help me?

- **"I really want your business?"**
  So does everybody else. Do you expect us to hand you the business just because you want it? What are you going to do to impact my bottom line?

- **"Our client list is extensive?"**
  The firm we just heard from before you showed up had an awesome client list.

- **"I've been our number one salesperson for five straight years?"**
  So what, how much money has that put in my pocket?

Take every piece of information in your presentation and visualize the prospect or client saying "So what? What does that mean to me and my business? How will you add value to my project?"

Know the answers before you present.

2. Use Stories, Examples and Anecdotes

Stories bring presentations to life. They make information relevant to the listener.

Stories, anecdotes and examples can elicit a range of emotions and reactions from your audience. They create visual images.

Most exceptional presenters have developed their storytelling ability to an enviable plateau. They use stories to stimulate the listeners' minds and to instill their message.

Use stories, examples and anecdotes at the start of your presentation or as a powerful way to end your speech.

3. Eye Contact Is an Essential Engagement Tool

When you meet someone for the first time who will not look you in the eye, what do you tend to think of that person?

- She's insincere.
- He's not interested in me.

- She has low self-esteem.
- I question his knowledge.
- I question her expertise.
- I'm not sure if I can trust him.
- She doesn't like me.
- He's lying.
- She's arrogant.
- He's shy.
- She's preoccupied.

In some cultures eye contact can be perceived as aggressive or disrespectful. This is especially true in Pacific Rim countries. Know your audience and adjust your delivery.

Look at your audience! Don't glance and dart around the room. Lock-on for three to four seconds. Allow yourself time to connect. Avoid the feeding bird syndrome. Watch a bird at a feeder. Its head is constantly whipping around checking for danger. Birds at feeders rarely look relaxed. The same is true with speakers. Their heads move back and forth as if on a swivel. If you sustain eye contact three to four seconds, it helps stabilize your head and also helps stabilize your body.

Lock-on to One and Connect with Many

If your audience is large, lock-on to individuals in various sections of the room. When you lock-on to one person, there are several others around that person who think you are looking at them as well.

A CEO client and I were talking about Bill Clinton's effectiveness as a presenter. He commented that when Bill Clinton establishes sustained eye contact with one individual, it feels as though he is connecting with many individuals. He was right.

Some people are more comfortable looking over the heads of the audience. This technique makes the presenter more comfortable but the audience wonders, "What the heck is he looking at?"

Pretend the person you're making eye contact with is the only person in the room. By doing so, you create a one-on-one feel to your presentation. The person you're looking at feels connected. Your delivery appears personal and conversational.

Be Generous – Share Your Eye Contact with All

A critical, yet common presentation blunder is to look exclusively at the person thought to be the decision-maker. By doing so, the presenter alienates the other people in the room. The nonverbal message says to the audience "You are not important."

How can we possibly know who makes the final decisions? Do we base it on job titles? Do we base it on who appears to be the most influential? Do we even know the decision-making process?

Even if we're correct in pinpointing the decision-maker, we don't necessarily know who else will influence the decision, or how much influence they have. When we leave the room, the decision-maker might turn to the group and ask, "What do you think?" If we've alienated the group, they will not have positive regards for us. They will have the same feelings about us that we have about people who don't look us in the eye: insincere, not interested, lying, arrogant or low self esteem.

Dateline: Los Angeles – A top-producing broker delivers a proposal. Her audience: the prospect's CEO, CFO and a Sr. VP. She did not win the business. She later found out that the Sr. VP felt that she had been arrogant, and she probably would not give them the attention they deserved. Reflecting on her meeting, the broker remembered looking at and talking to the CEO and CFO. She did not remember looking at or talking to the Sr. VP. She made the fatal mistake of thinking the CEO and CFO were the final decision-makers. In fact, the Sr. VP played a significant role in the decision.

The broker's lack of eye contact with the Sr. VP cost her a large commission and the opportunity to work with a company that will need additional services for years to come.

Common sense and common courtesy suggest that we share our eye contact. Respect every person in the room. Involve them.

Don't Gravitate to the Friendly Faces

It's possible that the unfriendly looking person is preoccupied with an upcoming project deadline. It's possible that they had a fight with their spouse earlier in the day. They could have been up all night with a sick child.

It's interesting that the person who looks least interested during a session will be the first to come up afterward and say how much she enjoyed the session. Makes me wonder what she looks like when she doesn't enjoy a session.

As you continue to share your eye contact with members of the audience, interesting conversions will take place. Audience members who refused to make eye contact early in the presentation will suddenly make sustained eye contact. People who had that, "I couldn't be more bored" look will suddenly look interested.

Position Yourself So That You Are the Focus of Attention

Because our eyes are drawn to movement, a conference room with a glass wall can be the kiss of death for a presentation. If your audience is facing the glass, you can be assured that they will look at every person who walks past the glass. The same person will walk by seven times and everyone will glance at her every time. Position yourself so that you and your visual aids are the focus of attention.

Practicing Eye Contact

Eye contact is the easiest of the skills to practice.

- Practice in every conversation. Lock-on for three to four seconds.

- Make note of who you tend to look at while presenting.

- Make note of where your eyes wander when you're not interested, when you disagree, when you're angry or when you're scrambling to respond to a question.

- When the pressure is on, hang tough. Don't break eye contact. Fleeing eyes reflect uncertainty and insecurity.

- Observe others under pressure. Watch their eyes. Do their eyes dart to the ceiling or to the floor? Do you sense poise or panic in their eyes?

- When conversing with a group at a business or networking function, share your eye contact with everyone.

- Practice with every handshake.

- Practice by giving others your undivided attention.

Develop a high level of comfort with eye contact. It is an essential tool to engaging your audience.

4. DON'T WASTE TIME TALKING TO INANIMATE OBJECTS

Fact: No screen, flip chart, dry erase board, floor, ceiling or conference table has <u>ever</u>, I repeat, <u>ever</u> made a decision.

Keep Your Shoulders Square to the Audience

There is a tendency for presenters who are using computer-generated visuals, flip charts, or dry erase boards to repeatedly glance at their visuals. Presenters can eat up chunks of time looking at their slides instead of looking at their audience. And the more presenters look at their visuals, the less familiar they appear with their material.

5. SMILE

A smile eases tension and creates a warm environment. A smile lights up one's eyes. A smile says, "I've done this before, I'm confident and I'll do my best to make this an interesting and informative session."

A smile indicates that you are:

- Relaxed
- Confident
- Approachable
- Prepared

Nervous people tend not to smile. People who are preoccupied or unprepared tend not to smile.

Don't hold your smile back. Show some teeth. If you say something that is intended to be funny, enjoy the moment. Keep your head and eyes up. If they laugh or smile, that's wonderful. If they don't, simply move on to your next point.

If you appear relaxed, your audience will relax. Audiences, for the most part, want the presenter to do well. They appreciate the work and preparation a presentation takes. Most people hope the material is interesting and informative. Most people are glad that it's you presenting and not them.

There are times when it is inappropriate to smile. You will most likely recognize these situations.

6. USE NAMES EARLY AND OFTEN

"Remember that a person's name is to that person the sweetest and most important sound in any language."

Dale Carnegie

It is important to mingle before meetings in order to meet and greet the audience. Learn their names. Find out their expectations. Introduce people to one another.

Make a Seating Chart

As people walk into the room, shake hands, introduce yourself, chat and then write down their names on your seating chart.

Use the seating chart to write down comments you heard prior to the meeting. Reference those comments during the meeting. If you have forgotten someone's name, ask for it again, "What is your name again?" Then use her name immediately.

Do not use a person's name as you look down at the seating chart. Look at the chart, talk for 20 seconds and then say, "Lynn, we discussed this issue prior to the meeting."

The use of names:
- Shows that you care.
- Builds rapport.
- Creates participation.
- Grabs their attention.
- Stops distracting conversations.

7. GET TO YOUR FEET

We're more persuasive on our feet than in our seat.

Own the Room is about being in control of what happens during your presentation. Getting to your feet enables you to take charge and control the flow of information. It allows you to change the dynamics of the room, create energy and assume a more commanding posture.

A study at the University of Minnesota concluded that if we stand up and present our information using some kind of visual aid, we are 43% more likely to persuade the listener.

What makes us more persuasive when we stand?
- We can make eye contact with everyone in the room.
- We speak from a position of authority and command.

- When a presenter stands up, people tend to look up.
- We can physically move closer to the audience.
- We are more easily seen and heard.
- Voice projection is enhanced.
- We're better able to use visual aids: a flip chart, dry erase board, map, photo, projected image or prop.
- Movement, animation and visuals create energy and lengthen attention spans.
- We can express ourselves more completely.

Eyes are instinctively drawn to movement. To maintain the attention of your audience, MOVE. Don't drift. Move with purpose and make movement meaningful. Create an active environment in which it is easy to pay attention.

It is difficult to pay attention to a one-dimensional presenter. One-dimensional means that the presenter sits down, doesn't use visuals and projects little, if any, animation. Just words, words, words.

Change the dynamics of the room. Stand up.

8. USE CURRENT EVENTS AND PERIODICALS

Incorporate current events or periodicals that tie directly to your message. By doing so, you create the impression that your information is fresh and that you are on top of what is happening in the world. It also demonstrates your effort to bring current and relevant information to your audience..

Speakers who deliver the same speech repeatedly appreciate this technique. Using that day's *New York Times*, for example, sounds fresh. It turns a canned speech into an impromptu speech. The more recent the event or the periodical, the greater the effect.

Use periodicals your audience is likely to be familiar with. Business groups for example relate to periodicals such as the *Wall Street Journal, Forbes, Fortune, Investor's Daily*, or *The Financial Times*.

If you want to grab the attention of an audience of accountants say, "How many of you have seen this month's issue of the *Journal of Accountancy*?" They will be favorably impressed, especially if you are not an accountant.

Magazines and newspaper articles can be a source of humor for your presentation. If you find something in an article to be funny, your audience will likely find it funny as well.

9. HUMOR

> *"Against the assault of laughter, nothing can stand."*
> Mark Twain

There is nothing like humor to break down barriers, build rapport and disarm opponents. Comedian/pianist Victor Borge once said, "Laughter is the shortest distance between two people."

During the 1984 presidential campaign, questions were raised about the impact of President Reagan's advancing age on his ability to lead. During a debate with Walter Mondale, the President was asked a question about age and the election. President Reagan responded, *"I refuse to make age an issue in this election. I will not exploit, for political purposes, the youth and inexperience of my opponent."*

Walter Mondale joined the audience in a hearty laugh and later admitted that Reagan's humorous response marked the end of any chance he had to win the election. Age took a back seat to other issues from that point forward.

Much has been written about humor through the years. If a proven formula for being funny existed, everyone would have it. Here are a few tips:

- It is hard to dislike someone with whom you find yourself laughing.

- Stories are better than jokes. Most have probably already heard your joke. It takes a great deal of practice and experience to be an effective joke teller.

  Tie the story to your message. If no one laughs, your message has still been delivered.

- Keep a journal of events, quotes, stories and situations you find amusing.

- Observe the people with whom you communicate most. What do they find funny?

- Draw from all sources (books, magazines, cartoons, TV, radio and conversations).

Adapt a quote to the occasion.

"I refuse to join any club that would have me as a member." Groucho Marx

"I refuse to live in a country that would elect me to public office." James Carville on *Imus In the Morning*

Quote Books Cover Virtually Any Topic

"I often quote myself. It adds spice to my conversation."
George Bernard Shaw

The Forbes Book of Business Quotations

The Reader's Digest Treasury of Modern Quotations

Speaker's Library of Business Stories, Anecdotes and Humor by Joe Griffith

Dictionary of Modern Quotations, J.M. and M.J Cohen

Using a quote off the cuff demonstrates a quick mind and in many cases, quick wit. Stay alert. Keep a log of quotes that will support your message or make them laugh.

Read Books on Comedy

Comedy Writing Secrets by Melvin Helitzer

How to Write and Sell Humor by Gene Perret

Comedy Writing Workbook by Gene Perret

There are numerous books filled with serious and humorous quotes from famous people:

The Kennedy Wit, Published by The Citadel Press

A Churchill Reader, The Wit and Wisdom of Sir Winston Churchill by Colin Coote

The Quotable Reagan by Peter Hannaford

10. READ YOUR AUDIENCE

By now you should be convinced that body language, movement, facial expressions and voice all send messages to your audience. Use your newly acquired knowledge to pick up messages being sent by your audience. Your audience will provide an abundance of feedback IF you watch for the messages they're sending.

Presenters who look at the floor, lock onto their notes or haphazardly pan the room miss an abundance of audience feedback. Be alert for the subtle glances, facial expressions, posture and physical reactions.

In an interview with Bryant Gumbel, comedian Jerry Seinfeld said that a comedy routine should be a dialogue rather than a monologue. He has to communicate with the audience even if he is doing all the talking.

People will glance at a decision-maker to see how she reacts to what is being said. Perhaps the presenter has hit on a sensitive issue.

Note the glances, frowns and smirks. Listen for the sighs. They mean something. If you see a reaction that indicates confusion or disagreement, address it. "Is everyone clear on that point?" or "Bill, do you agree with our premise?" or "Cathy, do you have any concerns thus far?"

By doing so, you accomplish three things: 1) you clear up any confusion or misunderstanding, 2) you get the audience involved and allow them to air feelings and comments, 3) you demonstrate that you are sensitive to the concerns of your audience.

Facial expressions can indicate agreement, disagreement, confusion, exhaustion and other emotions.

Eye contact and attention seem to go hand in hand. If you're losing their eye contact, you're probably losing their attention.

Is their body language open or closed? Are they leaning forward with interest? Are they stretching and yawning? Are they frequently adjusting in their seats, indicating discomfort?

Are they asking questions? Participating? Are they taking notes?

If your audience looks distracted, uninterested, bored, antsy or tired, they probably are. Change topics. Change the tempo. Move to different material. Take a break. Get them to stand and stretch. Ask someone for a comment. Get them involved.

The average amount of time that you have an adult's undivided attention is between 15 and 30 seconds. Audiences mentally drift in and out of presentations and conversations all the time. Don't take it as an insult if an audience member seems adrift. Attention spans are brief. It's your responsibility to do everything possible to maintain their interest.

When you look at someone in your audience, notice how he may appear to be looking back, but you're quite sure his mind is elsewhere. Seconds after you make eye contact, he shakes his head as if he has been driving a car for too many hours.

At a seminar last year I observed one of those head shakes from a gentleman sitting in the front row. I asked, "Where were you just then, Jeremy?" He answered, "Canoeing." He was going canoeing the following day.

Few, if any, presenters can hold the undivided attention of an audience for extended periods. But it is every presenter's responsibility to use all available tools and techniques to maintain the attention of the audience and make the presentation a productive experience.

Be alert for non-verbal communication from your audience. Although body language is not 100% accurate in predicting what someone is feeling, we should stay alert for the signals. Going the extra mile to engage your audience shows that you care. Listen to the body language of your audience and adjust your message and delivery accordingly.

We cannot determine the exact thoughts, moods or interests of an audience by watching body language. We can, however, pick up valuable clues as to how the audience feels.

Much has been written about body language. On the following pages, you will find common non-verbal indicators you can use to evaluate, in a non-scientific way, the mood of your audience.

ATTENTIVE AUDIENCE

Nodding head yes .... I agree, I understand

Sustained eye contact .... I'm following you

Sitting up/leaning forward .... I'm interested, tell me more

Smiling .... Engaged, enjoying the info

Laughing at subtle humor .... Tuned in

Comments and questions .... I want to be involved

Taking notes .... Eager to learn and remember

Relaxed posture .... Comfortable, open to info

INATTENTIVE OR BORED AUDIENCE

Sparse eye contact .... Interest is waning

Head held up by hands .... Bored, tired

Rubbing eyes .... Ready to move on

Shifting in seat, fidgeting .... Antsy, mentally moving on

Yawns .... Tired, bored or nervous

Arms and legs crossed .... Closed off, not buying it

Head and eyes down .... Mentally somewhere else

Picking lint off clothes .... This is getting tedious

Eyes wandering around room ...... Tell me something new

Blank stare .... Daydreaming, adios

GENERAL SIGNS OF NERVOUSNESS OR DISCOMFORT

- Avoiding eye contact.
- Clearing throat repeatedly.
- Fidgety hands – scratching, playing with pen.
- Speaking rapidly.
- Sound winded when speaking.
- Perspiration under arms.
- Rapid leg bounce.
- Chewing objects such as pens, fingers.
- Twirling hair.
- More hesitation in their speech.
- More mispronounced words.
- Higher pitched voice.
- Voice "cracking."
- Defensive in responses. Guarded.
- Shifting frequently in their seat.
- Awkward or sudden smiles, giggles or laughs.

11. GET YOUR AUDIENCE INVOLVED

*"I hear and I forget, I see and I remember,
I do and I understand."*
Chinese proverb

If you want people to remember your message, get them involved. Encourage participation. If they hear, see and participate in the development of the message, they will certainly walk away retaining much more than if you simply lecture to them.

Audience members who expect to participate pay closer attention than those who know their involvement will not be encouraged.

Techniques for involvement:

- State up front that audience participation is expected.

- Ask them questions.

- Use the phrase, "Write this down" followed by a list.

- Use props: maps, flipcharts, dry erase boards, products, drawings.

- Use an outline that requires the audience to fill in the blanks.

- Distance – get to your feet in order to get closer to the audience. It is difficult to ignore someone who is squared up to you, looking you straight in the eye.

  **Be alert not to violate personal space.

- Use audience members in your stories and examples.

- Use names.

- Ask their opinion.

- Conduct a survey.

- Have them raise their hands. "How many of you have ever...?

- Group discussions.

- Periodicals – share something current and relevant. Don't pass it around lest you will immediately lose their attention.

- Use video clips that match your message. Humorous clips can be especially effective.

- Periodically reward someone for a response or comment.

CHAPTER SEVEN

Natural

Exceptional presenters are natural. Their style is conversational, and they look completely at ease in front of any audience.

A presentation by a natural presenter sounds lively, it flows easily, and though it is well rehearsed, it does not sound scripted. Natural is making it look like you've done it a 1000 times before. Natural presenters are fluid, their eye contact is engaging, and their voice is easy to listen to.

By natural, I do not mean, someone who was born a naturally exceptional presenter. Exceptional presenters achieve that status by working at it and practicing the art of presenting. In the years I have been coaching, booking and researching speakers, I have yet to come across a single exceptional presenter who said they were exceptional from the beginning.

Make a list of presenters you would classify as "natural" and describe what you believe makes them natural?

_____

_____

_____

_____

_____

_____

CHAPTER EIGHT

Understand Your Audience

New York Stock Exchange Rule 405:
Exchange members must attempt to learn essential facts
about every customer and account. General guidelines
suggest the registered representative should know each
customer's present holdings, financial situation, risk
tolerance, needs and objectives.

Stockbrokers are required to "know the customer" prior to making any investment recommendations. If they fail to do so, brokers run the risk of fines, loss of license, or worse.

Just as stockbrokers must abide by Rule 405 NYSE, presenters should abide by presentation Rule 1:

Understand your audience.

Tips to Learn More About Your Audience

Speak to the issues, concerns, goals and fears that are important to your audience.

- Talk with people within the organization.

- Ask lots of questions.

- Listen for information you can build into your presentation.

- Do your homework. Research.

- Read their marketing material and brochures.

- Browse their web site.

- Use an Internet search engine for info on individuals who will attend.

- Peruse annual reports for company values, mission statement, performance numbers...

- Scan periodicals for information pertaining to the company or its' competitors.

- Watch for television reports.

- Visit their stores or offices.

- Get a copy of their most recent newsletter.

- Ask about terminology they dislike or avoid.

- Peruse local business journals.

Questions to Ask

- Who will be in attendance? How many? Get a list of names, titles, roles and responsibilities.

- Will the decision-makers be in the room?

- What are their expectations? What needs to be done to meet their expectations?

- What is the meeting theme?

- What agenda items come before and after your remarks?

- What is the expected attire? Is it formal, business, business casual or casual. When asking about attire, be sure to find out as much as you can. Business casual can mean different things to different groups. Casual to some is wool slacks, jackets and ties.

- Do the attendees get along? Do they laugh easily?

- What are the starting and ending times for the meeting?
- What is the seating arrangement and can it be changed?
- Is it a neutral, friendly or hostile audience?
- What do they know about your topic?
- What do they know about you, the presenter?

Researching and asking questions takes less time than you might think. It could take a couple of hours, but your work will pay big dividends.

In two or three phone calls, you can ask all of the questions listed above. In many cases, they will volunteer additional information. Be as conversational and curious as possible when asking the questions. Try not to make it sound like an interrogation. State up front that you need the information to ensure a productive meeting. Most organizations are happy to provide the information. They too want the meeting to be productive.

Your Introduction Is Important

An effective introduction should:
- Build the credibility of the speaker.
- Create anticipation for the speaker and her topic.
- Heighten the relevance of the topic to the audience.
- Be as brief as possible. Let the speaker speak.

Most introductions are ineffective. Most people don't introduce others often and they don't spend the appropriate time preparing.

When you are the speaker:

Type your introduction in paragraph form, using a font size

that is easy to read, 18 to 22. Send your introduction to the person who is scheduled to introduce you. Call that person to see if he needs any clarification and to have him read your introduction back to you. This prevents the awkward moment when he completely hacks up your name in front of the audience.

The introduction should help the audience understand who you are and why it's important for them to listen carefully to your information.

When you are introducing someone:

Ask the speaker to write out his introduction. Then read it back to him. Do the introduction justice by practicing it at least five times. Highlight facts that the speaker deems relevant. Be as brief as possible.

If you are unable to get a written introduction from the speaker, prepare the introduction yourself. Include <u>The 3Ps of Introductions</u>.

1) Professional background of the speaker - title, honors, awards, experience.

2) Personal background - family, hobbies, personal connection with you or the audience.

3) Purpose in speaking - relevance of the topic to the audience.

Deliver your introduction in a conversational manner. Never read the entire introduction with your head and eyes down. Look at the audience during the introduction. There is a tendency to look repeatedly at the speaker as if to make sure the information being delivered is accurate.

CHAPTER NINE

Practice

"We are what we repeatedly do.
Excellence, then, is not an act, but a habit."
Aristotle

If I cannot persuade you to practice, I cannot help you to improve.

The skills discussed in this book are quite basic. Mastering these skills is a matter of making them habits. Once they become habit, they will not fail you, even under the most extreme pressure and the most adverse circumstances.

When placed in pressure situations, our bodies seek comfort. If you are most comfortable with your hands in your pockets, that is where your hands will go when an audience member nails you with a tough question. If you are most comfortable looking down at the floor while thinking, that is where your eyes will go when a client asks you to justify your fees.

"No matter who you are,
no matter how good an athlete
you are, we're creatures of habit.
The better your habits are, the better
they'll be in pressure situations."
Hockey great Wayne Gretsky

*"Every great shot you hit, you've already hit
a bunch of times in practice."*

Martina Navratilova,
winner of 167 singles tennis titles,
including a record nine at Wimbledon

Practice is a critical component of being successful in any field of endeavor.

Amanda Borden was Captain of the 1996 Olympics Gold Medal USA Gymnastics team. Her training for a single event, such as the balance beam, included over 5000 repetitions of the entire routine and over 100,000 repetitions of the various skills (hand movements, turns, dismount...)

Janet Evans, three time Olympian and winner of four Olympic gold medals in swimming, swam twelve miles a day, six days a week during her twelve-year Olympic pursuit. That's approximately 45,000 miles of practice.

Byron Janise is renowned internationally as one of the world's greatest concert pianists. He once stated that if he missed one day of practice, he could tell. If he missed two days of practice, his coach could tell. If he missed three days of practice, his audience could tell.

The exciting thing about practicing these skills is that you don't need an audience. You don't need props. You don't need equipment. The only thing you need is the desire to improve.

Throughout this book I have listed practice opportunities that you can include in your normal daily routines. If you take advantage of the opportunities, you will improve quickly. If you don't take advantage of the opportunities, then these skills will NEVER become second nature. They will NEVER become part of your presentation arsenal.

The stronger your habits, the more consistent and effective you will be under the pressure of presenting and conducting question and answer sessions.

Repetition is critical but does not always guarantee improvement. As John Kilcullen, founder of the *For Dummies* books said,

> *"Just because you're doing something a lot, doesn't mean you're getting better. You might simply be reinforcing bad habits."*

Practice doesn't make perfect. Perfect practice makes perfect.

Exercise:

Write down the approximate percentage of your working day that you spend communicating and presenting. This includes conversations, meetings, phone calls, voice mail and every other venue in which you are speaking or listening.

Communicating _____ %

Now, write down the approximate percentage of time you spend practicing to improve your communication skills.

Practicing _____ %

When participants in my workshops fill out their percentages, I typically see the following results:

Communicating – the average response is 50% to 80%.

Practicing – the average response is 0% to 2%.

Most people spend absolutely no time practicing. Yet they communicate 50-80% of the time.

Following and in the back of the book are weekly practice charts. Begin today to document where, what and how often you practice. The more you practice, the sooner you will become exceptional.

DELIVERY SKILLS
WEEKLY PRACTICE CHART

SKILL SETS PRACTICED

Week of: _____
Note where you practiced.

	Posture	Gestures	Eye Contact	Voice Volume	Inflection	Filler	
Monday Comments:							
Tuesday Comments:							
Wednesday Comments:							
Thursday Comments:							
Friday Comments:							
Saturday Comments:							
Sunday Comments:							

Additional observations:

Who impressed you with their skills? _____

Why? _____

Who did not impress you? _____

Why? _____

CHAPTER TEN

Quick on Your Feet

Conducting Successful Q&A Answer Sessions

If your presentation is to be a success, then your question and answer session (Q&A) must be conducted professionally.

Q&A is an opportunity to build rapport, find out what is on the minds of your audience members, and share material you didn't have time to build into your presentation.

The credibility of a presenter can rise or fall during Q&A.

Q&A is perhaps the most significant segment of your presentation. During Q&A, you will find out if your message is getting through. Are they interested? Do they agree or disagree with your position? Are they engaged? A strong presentation can be overshadowed by a less than stellar Q&A session. In fact, it wasn't a strong presentation if the Q&A flopped.

In many situations your presentation will be a rolling Q&A session. People will ask questions throughout most presentations. Encouraging questions during the presentation can be effective, but it requires greater attention to time constraints. If your presentation is to last 10 minutes, it's a good idea to ask the audience to hold their questions until the end. A 3-minute question in the middle of a 10-minute presentation can make a significant dent in the amount of material you are able to cover. It can also break your momentum and divert the flow of information.

Let's approach Q&A from a position of strength and experience rather than surprise and retreat.

Q&A Tips and Techniques

Composure, Composure, Composure

Maintain your composure at all times. We tend to react adversely to the unknown or the unexpected. We can never be totally prepared for every question, but we can anticipate questions and practice our responses to those questions.

By maintaining your composure, you are able to think clearly and respond appropriately. If you lose your cool, you will most likely lose credibility with the audience.

It is critical during Q&A that your non-verbal skills are strong and second nature. Our natural response to pressure is to move away from the source of pressure.

Maintain a "move forward" attitude during Q&A sessions. Do not retreat. Maintain strong body language. This is especially true when the questions become more difficult or more aggressive.

Read Your Audience

Watch the body language, facial expressions, voice projection and inflection of the person asking the question. If you are observant, you can get a good feel for the intent of the question. Is she asking the question because she is confused? Does she need clarification? Is she challenging me with the question? Is she eager to hear more?

By watching body language and listening to tone of voice, you can quickly discern a friendly question from a hostile question. You can distinguish a question based on misunderstanding from a question based on curiosity.

Rehearse, Rehearse, Rehearse

Conduct mock Q&A sessions prior to your presentation. Ask members of your organization to play the role of the audience. Have them fire questions at you from all angles. Encourage them to hit you with the toughest possible questions. Encourage them to challenge your responses. Practice rapid-fire, unfair and uninformed questions. Convince one person to play the audience jerk. You'll probably have several volunteers for that role.

If you don't have a group available to help you conduct a mock Q&A, write down questions on 3X5 cards, shuffle the cards and answer the questions as they are dealt. Practice as if it were the real Q&A. If you will be standing during your presentation, then stand when you practice. Work the room as if it were the actual presentation. Practice moving toward your audience. Practice repeating and rephrasing questions. Work on your eye contact (even if the eye contact is with chairs when you practice). The more accurately you can simulate the Q&A, the more effective you will be when you go live.

Mock sessions are worth their weight in gold. Answers tend to be smoother when we've said them two or three times. How we think about an answer and how we actually verbalize that answer can be surprisingly different.

Politicians spend a considerable amount of time preparing for debates. They understand that a single response can make or break the debate and possibly make or break the election.

Know Your Audience

The more you know about your audience, the better prepared you will be for Q&A.

Respect Your Audience

Respect all questions. Even when you're sure you're right and the audience member is wrong, don't go for the jugular. It's not worth the short lived gratification. Your ego will be gratified, but your credibility will be tarnished. Earn respect by respecting others and by handling an unprofessional attack with poise and professionalism.

Take Charge

Stand your ground with the calm and presence of a seasoned professional.

Q&A Reminders

The best thing you can do to ensure a successful Q&A is to effectively frame your presentation when you first begin speaking. By doing so, you start with a clear purpose, you can stay on point and you can redirect off-topic questions.

- Encourage participation.

- Understand the question, or don't answer the question. Ask for clarification, ask the person to define part of the question, request that the person give you an example to illustrate the question, or turn to the other members of the group to see if they could help you understand the question.

- Multiple part questions. Answer questions one part at a time. Don't burden yourself by trying to remember and then answer a three or four part question. Break down the question. "What was part one of your question?" Answer part one and move on to part two of the question, part three...

  If you are asked a three-part question, choose the part you want to respond to first. This gives you additional time to think about your responses to the other parts of the question.

- Repeat or rephrase the question.

  "Let me make sure I understand your question."
  "If I understand your question, you're asking me…"
  "The question, for those who did not hear it was…."
  "It sounds like you're concerned with the adoption of the…"

- Involve everyone. Repeat and answer the question to the entire group. DO NOT answer the entire question with your eye contact solely fixed on the person who asked the question. Presenters who do this tend to lose the rest of the audience.

- At the end of an answer, ask the questioner, "Does that answer your question?" You may not want to use this technique if the person asking the questions has been a burr in your Q&A saddle. Simply move on to the next question.

- Stay in control! Keep the information relevant. Don't allow an audience member to change the direction of your presentation and Q&A. The more defined you are at the beginning of your presentation about the topic and your objectives, the easier it is to cut off questions that don't match those objectives.

- Keep it simple. Answer the question and move on. Don't dwell, don't ramble, don't try to tell them everything you know.

- Use names to personalize your answers. "Brenda's question has to do with…" "Jeff asked a question regarding…"

- Maintain strong body language. Move forward and maintain eye contact, even on the toughest, most aggressive questions. Don't retreat.

- Be aware of your eye contact. Lock-on to the questioner while she asks the question. Avoid glancing at the ceiling or the floor. Eyes speak volumes as to one's confidence level. Try to maintain eye contact as you respond.

- Don't fidget, dance, shuffle or get defensive. Keep your cool. They might simply be testing to see how you react.

- Neutralize a negative question. Question: "Why are your fees so ridiculously high?" Response: "Your question has to do with how we structure our fees, let me..."

- Be alert for questions you are not qualified to answer. It's a bad idea to answer legal questions if you are not an attorney or tax questions if you lack the credentials. Some people feel compelled to respond even if they are not qualified.

- If you don't know, don't bluff. Set it up early in your presentation that you might not have all the answers to all of their questions right now. You will, however, find the answers and get back with them. Give them a specific time frame in which you will get back with the answer. This builds credibility.

If you are caught bluffing, simply pack your bags and depart. You will have little if any credibility with the audience.

Dateline: San Jose, CA – A participant in a CEO boot camp told me that he ALWAYS comes up with an answer, whether he has one or not. I asked him if he has ever been caught bluffing. He said he had been caught bluffing one time.

He was delivering a funding presentation to a group of venture capitalists (VCs). Five minutes into the presentation one of the VCs interrupted saying, "Ed, did you know that Microsoft is developing this same technology? How can you begin to compete with Microsoft?" Our CEO was caught off guard. He had no idea that Microsoft was developing a similar product. But that didn't stop him from trying to bluff his way through a response. He launched into a comparison of his company's technology and Microsoft's technology. His product was better because of this, this and this. Microsoft's doesn't do this, this and this.

Three minutes into Ed's response the VC spoke up again. "You know what? I was thinking about a different technology. Microsoft isn't developing anything like your product."

Oops! Ed was caught in a bluff. For three minutes he compared his product to a phantom product. Everyone in the room knew he was bluffing. He had entered the room hoping to secure a $2,000,000 investment. He left the room with the exact amount of money he had in his wallet at the start of the meeting.

Bluffing destroys trust. Don't do it.

Buying Time to Gather Your Thoughts

There are times when you need a few seconds to think about an answer before responding. You might need 15 to 30 seconds to formulate an appropriate response. It is better to stop and think than to begin your answer hemming and hawing until you finally find your direction. Your audience will know you're dancing, and your answer will have less impact.

Take your time. The human brain can sort through an incredible amount of information in three to five seconds if you maintain your composure and let it work. Resist the urge to fill the air with words that are yet to be formed into a cohesive thought.

- Pause. This is your most powerful tool. Use it. Pausing to think through your response is a sign that you are reflecting on the question. Think through your response. Be consistent. Pause whether the question is difficult or easy.

*"Silence is golden when you
can't think of a good answer."*
Muhammad Ali, More Than a Hero

Three seconds of silence to a nervous speaker feels like an eternity. Three seconds of silence to a confident speaker feels natural.

Former President Bill Clinton is a master of the pause. Think back to the 1992 and 1996 presidential debates. Bill Clinton would pause with every question. It didn't matter if the question was difficult or easy. He would pause, move toward the person asking the question and then respond.

- The extended pause comes into play when you realize that it will take at least ten seconds to formulate your response. Let your audience know that you are going to think through your response. Take as much time as you need. "Let me think about that before I respond."

  A pause is a sign of confidence. Many people cannot handle silence when they are expected to be speaking or responding.

- Repeat or rephrase the question as a courtesy to others in the room. "Let me make sure I understand your question..." "If I understand your question, you're asking me..." "Allow me to repeat your question." "For those who did not hear the question, it had to do with..."

- Ask the questioner to repeat the question. Limit the use of this technique. Save it for when you truly do not hear the question. If overused, it can appear an obvious stall tactic. It can also give the impression that the presenter is not intelligent enough to understand the question the first time through.

- Return to the topic later. "Let's come back to that later." "Kim, remind me to revisit that after the break." "If you could hold that question, we'll be covering that topic in the next segment."

- Open the question to the group. Use when appropriate (training, seminars, situations where you are trying to encourage participation). It would not be appropriate, for example, in a proposal situation as you present to the CEO, CFO and Senior VP. "OK, Bill asked the question, why are our fees so ridiculously high. Does anyone want to respond to that question?"

- Ask them a question. "What did you do in that situation?" "Amy, does your question pertain to our discussion yesterday?"

- Find out why they are asking the question. "And the reason you are asking that question?" "Specifically what would you like to know?" "And your question is?" "Why do you ask?" It is important when using this technique to use the appropriate tone of voice. Use a tone of voice that implies that you are doing your best to discern what they would like to know.

- Ask them to define part of the question. "Jill, define for me what you meant by the word *variables*."

- Take a sip of water. Try not to take your first sip of water immediately after hearing a difficult question.

- Take a break if the timing is right.

Team Presentations and Q&A

Determine who will answer questions on specific topics during your rehearsals. Don't stare at each other waiting for your teammate to answer a question.

If you're going to direct a question to a member of your team, first say the name of the team member to whom you are directing the question. This alerts the person just in case they've been napping. Repeat the question in order to give your teammate time to formulate her response.

Make your teammates look good. Do not correct them in a way that can remotely be interpreted as condescending. Partners have been known to destroy the credibility of managers by stepping in and correcting the manager in front of the client. Sometimes the correction is necessary in order to avoid misstating the situation. But tone of voice, body language and word choice make the difference between the manager feeling OK about the correction or feeling completely crushed.

Exceptional Q&A:
British Prime Minister Tony Blair

Few people communicate as effectively in Q&A sessions as Tony Blair. Tune into any press conference featuring the Prime Minister and you will see what I mean.

Tony Blair exudes enthusiasm and professionalism. He radiates confidence and speaks in a conversational tone, even when reading a script. His message rings of optimism. He gestures freely and effectively. He smiles readily. Any and all questions are welcome. He stands tall and always stands his ground. His eye contact is direct and he shares it with as much of the audience as possible.

It is rare to hear Tony Blair utter an "um" or "uh." People with a clear and well-defined message typically do not use "verbal graffiti." He is as effective off the cuff as he is off a script.

Prime Minister Blair has a good sense of humor and will use it to build rapport, disarm an adversary or keep an opponent off balance. Anyone who has watched Tony Blair during Prime Minister's Questions on C-SPAN understands the need to be "quick on your feet" and possess a quick wit during these House of Commons sessions.

Prime Minister Blair is one of the most animated, dynamic and effective presenters of our time. People often ask me who they can watch to observe exceptional presentation skills in action. Watch Tony Blair.

Secretary of Defense Donald Rumsfeld

Tune into a Pentagon briefing and it is clear that Secretary Donald Rumsfeld is in complete control. He is always well-prepared. He knows what he will discuss, what he cannot discuss and what he will not discuss.

His sense of confidence can be seen in his posture: standing erect with his head and eyes up. His eye contact is sustained and unflinching. He will squint while listening as if to demonstrate his undivided attention.

He is quick to:

- Correct inaccuracies, "I didn't say that."

- Correct false assumptions, "It would be a mistake for you to assume anything from what I just said other than what I just said."

- Correct inaccurate conclusions, "I think you're making a mistake to draw a conclusion."

He will defer questions until later in the briefing if he is not prepared to answer immediately.

Secretary Rumsfeld's approach to a friendly question is the same as his approach to a hostile question: respectful and professional.

The Secretary appears relaxed and reflective. He pauses as long as he needs to formulate his response. His movements and gestures are open, specific and descriptive.

Donald Rumsfeld approaches each briefing from a position of strength and experience.

CHAPTER ELEVEN

Using Nervous Energy to Create Positive Results

"Public speaking is one of the best things I hate."
Baseball great Yogi Berra

S weaty palms, beads on your forehead and upper lip, racing pulse, tight stomach, dry mouth, shortness of breath, wobbly knees, shaking hands, sudden lapses of memory, and the impulse to flee. Isn't public speaking fun?

It has long been said that public speaking is listed as the number one fear in the *Book of Lists*. Many people would rather be stung repeatedly by a swarm of killer bees than to stand up and deliver a speech.

Comedian Jerry Seinfeld suggests that the next time you attend a funeral, think about this: the person in the coffin is more relaxed than the person who has to deliver the eulogy.

Nervousness is a reaction to pressure and our desire to perform to the best of our ability. Ask any world class performer in any field of endeavor, and the vast majority will admit that they get nervous prior to a performance. It's the competitive drive, the will to win and the fear of failure.

Why do we get nervous prior to, and sometimes during, a presentation? Presenting to a group is not something most people do every day. Fear of failure. The possibility of sounding incompetent can make anyone apprehensive. If you are a professional, you want to perform to your highest level. There's always a chance that during your presentation, you will:

- Fall on your face – literally or figuratively.
- Make a major gaffe.
- Freeze up and forget your message.
- Face an audience member who knows more about your topic than you.
- Be stumped by questions from the audience.

You're Not Different – Most People Get Nervous

- Mikhail Baryshnikov, perhaps the world's most renowned dancer, admitted that he gets so nervous before performances, he feels physically ill. He doesn't know why. He can't stand the fact that it happens. But it happens.
- Lifelong actress Helen Hayes said that the day she didn't get nervous before a performance would be the day she would retire. If she reached a point where she wasn't nervous, it meant that she did not care enough about the audience.
- Johnny Carson said he was nervous every night prior to his *Tonight Show* monologue. He did over 4000 shows.

The Mental Game of Presenting

Many people claim that presenting makes them feel like they're standing in a spotlight. All eyes trained on their every move. Any mistake will be noted and archived in a permanent record.

Take comfort in knowing that most audiences are not paying THAT close of attention to your presentation. Remember that the average adult attention span is 15-30 seconds.

Focus the Spotlight on Your Message and Your Audience

Approach your presentation with the mindset that, "This message is important to this group. I will do everything in my power to help them understand and remember the message."

This mindset enables you to direct your energy to bringing out the message. It also enables you to assist the audience in understanding what you have to say.

It's not about you. It's about the message.

Mental approach:

Option A – Oh my gosh, every eye in the place is staring at me. I have to stand here for thirty minutes and speak to this group.

Option B – I have critical information that can make a positive difference for the people in this room. I have thirty minutes to help them understand this information. Let's get started.

Convert Nervous Energy to Positive Energy

Pre-presentation nerves are what drive us to prepare more than we would if we were totally relaxed approaching a presentation. Nervousness keeps us alert and provides a boost of adrenaline.

Work to channel your nervous energy into crisp, well - defined gestures and movements. Convert your nervous energy to greater voice projection and inflection. Tap your nervous energy to encourage participation so you are not standing in the spotlight, but shining the spotlight on everyone in the room.

Techniques for Controlling the Fear

Two-minute Drill

Memorize your first two minutes. I don't necessarily mean word for word. Practice your first two minutes repeatedly until they flow smoothly. The exact words may change slightly with each attempt, but your message is clear and consistent.

Feeling completely comfortable that your opening is solid and secure will be a tremendous help in calming the jitters.

Cheat Sheets

If you need to have notes nearby or with you, by all means do so. You don't have to rely completely on your memory. If you do carry notes, however, don't lock your eyes onto your notes and become dependent on them throughout your presentation.

Rehearse, Rehearse, Rehearse

There is no substitute for rehearsal. Rehearse out loud. Visualize your audience in front of you while you rehearse. If you will be using visual aids, use them as you rehearse.

Rehearse in Three-minute Segments

Rehearsing your presentation from start to finish can get tiresome quickly. The start to finish method also allows fewer opportunities to adjust and adapt your material. Break the presentation into three-minute segments. Work on each segment multiple times. Be sure to work on your transitions from one segment to the next.

This approach will allow you to refine the material. It will also enable you to adjust the content on the fly. You can easily remove segments that you find do not apply to your audience. You can skip ahead to a specific segment if a question pertaining to that segment is asked. The segmented approach also allows you to keep more accurate track of how your presentation times out.

It's OK to Forget

Lapses of memory happen to the very best performers. Don't let it throw you. Assume that you will have an occasional memory lapse or "brain cramp." Pause, glance down at your notes, gather your thoughts, look up and continue your presentation.

Don't Try to Tell Them Everything You Know

There is a tendency for people to feel like they need to pass along every detail of their topic to anyone willing to listen. People don't want to know everything you know. Keep it simple. If they want more detail, they will ask for it.

Reduce your material – If your presentation is scheduled to last 20 minutes, don't try to deliver 25 minutes of material. Be prepared with 17 minutes of material and allow time for flexibility and spontaneity. Believe me, no one will complain if you finish 2 minutes early.

Don't feel compelled to cover every item in detail during your presentation. That's why there's Q&A. Q&A allows you to touch on material you were unable to cover in the allotted time.

Arrive an Hour Early

Give yourself time to prepare and relax. Remember our 60-20 Rule. Arrive 60 minutes early so that you can relax. Meet and greet for the 20 minutes prior to your presentation.

Mingle

Meet as many participants as possible. Build some allies prior to your presentation.

Visualize Success

Picture yourself delivering an exceptional speech.

Breathe Deeply

Deep breathing helps relax your body.

Take a Walk – Get Some Exercise

Studies show that exercise can help to relax your system for two hours or more following the exercise. Take a brisk walk prior to departing for your presentation.

Be Yourself

We all have different presentation styles. Don't try to be someone else. Let your personality flow. I have witnessed presenters who feel compelled to be funny because the presenter before them was funny. Don't force it! As President George Bush, Sr. used to say, "Stay the course." Be yourself. Stick with your style and your material.

Be Careful What You Eat and Drink

Because nervousness ties stomachs in knots and makes mouths dry, avoid:

- **Eating a large meal just prior to presenting**: It's better to have your blood flowing to your brain during the presentation than having your body's energy directed to digesting that 22-ounce flank steak you just engulfed. Nervousness and a full stomach can add up to trouble.

- **Caffeine**: It affects different people different ways. If you are nervous or edgy, the last thing you want is to multiply that edge with a dose of caffeine.

- **Carbonated drinks**: When it comes to carbonation, what goes down must come up.

- **Ice water or cold drinks:** Your throat should be kept warm and moist. Because cold drinks tighten the throat, the safest drink is room temperature water. Decaffeinated tea, coffee, and hot chocolate are also good choices.

- **Dairy products:** In addition to potential intolerance dairy drinks tend to disturb the normal flow of fluids in our mouths. They tend to glob our fluids together and make it difficult to enunciate.

- **Fruit juices that are highly acidic**: If it sounds like the presenter has something caught in her throat, chances are good that she is drinking cranberry juice, lemonade, orange juice or another form of fruit drink.

Do Not Accept Average When You Can Be Exceptional

*"Once you fly, you will walk
with your eyes skyward. For there you
have been and there you will go again."*
Leonardo da Vinci

Congratulations on completing the first part of your journey to becoming an exceptional presenter. What you do from this point will determine how quickly you reach the exceptional level. As you will soon come to see, improving your ability to present and persuade will affect every aspect of your life.

Please remember three things:

1) Do not accept average when you can be exceptional.

2) Every contact counts. Every interview counts. Every presentation counts.

3) Those who practice improve. Those who don't, don't.

Once you achieve exceptional,
you will never again accept average.

Good luck.

Visit my web site at www.theexceptionalpresenter.com. You will find updated techniques, success stories, and information pertaining to the art of presenting. Share your thoughts on this book, your presentation experiences and your success stories.

Begin your journey to exceptional today by establishing your personal improvement goals on the following page. Then, objectively assess progress after each presentation by completing the Presentation Assessment Form that follows the Improvement Goals sheet.

*   *   *   *   *

To order additional copies of
The Exceptional Presenter, visit
www.theexceptionalpresenter.com

PERSONAL IMPROVEMENT GOALS

Today's Date: **Scale 1-10 (9-10 Being Exceptional)**

Overall Rating _____

How can I improve my overall rating?

_____

_____

Date of:	Noticeable Improvement	Significant Improvement	Exceptional
Presence			
Posture			
Gestures 2nd Nature			
Eye Contact Shared and Sustained			
Movement – Visuals			
Voice Projection			
Inflection			
Filler Free			
Overall Effectiveness			

Game plan for achieving my improvement goals

_____

_____

PRESENTATION ASSESSMENT FORM

(Rating scale: 1 = not at all; 10 = exceptional)

Presentation:

Was I **organized**? (1-10) _____

Strengths and deficiencies of my content? _____

Was my delivery **passionate**? (1-10) _____

Primary posture: (circle one or more):

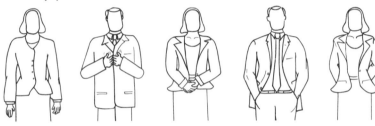

Gestures and movement: Defined, nebulous or limited

Eye contact: Sustained for three to four seconds? Y N
            Shared – Did I involve everyone? Y N

Facial expressions: Open and inviting or reserved

_____

Voice: Dynamic or monotone? •
         (Chart your range)   _____

Verbal graffiti / filler used: _____

Was I **engaging**? (1-10) _____

Engagement techniques used: _____

Was I **natural** and conversational? (1-10) _____

Overall rating (1-10, 10 being best): _____

Additional comments and observations: _____

PRESENTATION ASSESSMENT FORM

(Rating scale: 1 = not at all; 10 = exceptional)

Presentation:

Was I **organized**? (1-10) _____

Strengths and deficiencies of my content? _____

_____

Was my delivery **passionate**? (1-10) _____

Primary posture: (circle one or more):

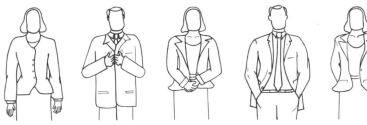

Gestures and movement: Defined, nebulous or limited

Eye contact: Sustained for three to four seconds? Y N

Shared – Did I involve everyone?   Y N

Facial expressions: Open and inviting or reserved

_____

Voice: Dynamic or monotone?   •

(Chart your range)   _____

Verbal graffiti / filler used: _____

Was I **engaging**? (1-10) _____

Engagement techniques used: _____

Was I **natural** and conversational? (1-10) _____

Overall rating (1-10, 10 being best): _____

Additional comments and observations: _____

_____

PRESENTATION ASSESSMENT FORM

(Rating scale: 1 = not at all; 10 = exceptional)

Presentation:

Was I **organized**? (1-10) _____

Strengths and deficiencies of my content? _____

Was my delivery **passionate**? (1-10) _____

Primary posture: (circle one or more):

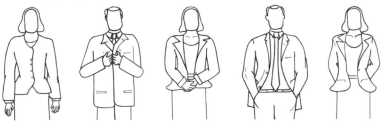

Gestures and movement: Defined, nebulous or limited

Eye contact: Sustained for three to four seconds? Y N
　　　　　　　 Shared – Did I involve everyone?　Y N

Facial expressions: Open and inviting or reserved

_____

Voice:　Dynamic or monotone?　●
　　　　(Chart your range)　_____

Verbal graffiti / filler used: _____

Was I **engaging**? (1-10) _____

Engagement techniques used: _____

Was I **natural** and conversational? (1-10) _____

Overall rating (1-10, 10 being best): _____

Additional comments and observations: _____

DELIVERY SKILLS
WEEKLY PRACTICE CHART

SKILL SETS PRACTICED

Week of: _____
Note where you practiced.

	Posture	Gestures	Eye Contact	Voice Volume	Inflection	Filler	
Monday Comments:							
Tuesday Comments:							
Wednesday Comments:							
Thursday Comments:							
Friday Comments:							
Saturday Comments:							
Sunday Comments:							

Additional observations:

Who impressed you with their skills? _____

Why? _____

Who did not impress you? _____

Why? _____

DELIVERY SKILLS
WEEKLY PRACTICE CHART

SKILL SETS PRACTICED

Week of: _____
Note where you practiced.

	Posture	Gestures	Eye Contact	Voice Volume	Inflection	Filler	
Monday Comments:							
Tuesday Comments:							
Wednesday Comments:							
Thursday Comments:							
Friday Comments:							
Saturday Comments:							
Sunday Comments:							

Additional observations:

Who impressed you with their skills? _____

Why? _____

Who did not impress you? _____

Why? _____

DELIVERY SKILLS
WEEKLY PRACTICE CHART

SKILL SETS PRACTICED

Week of: _____

Note where you practiced.

Skill columns: Posture, Gestures, Eye Contact, Voice Volume, Inflection, Filler

	Posture	Gestures	Eye Contact	Voice Volume	Inflection	Filler
Monday Comments:						
Tuesday Comments:						
Wednesday Comments:						
Thursday Comments:						
Friday Comments:						
Saturday Comments:						
Sunday Comments:						

Additional observations:

Who impressed you with their skills? _____

Why? _____

Who did not impress you? _____

Why? _____

DELIVERY SKILLS
WEEKLY PRACTICE CHART

SKILL SETS PRACTICED

Week of: _____
Note where you practiced.

Skill columns: Posture, Gestures, Eye Contact, Voice Volume, Inflection, Filler

	Posture	Gestures	Eye Contact	Voice Volume	Inflection	Filler	
Monday Comments:							
Tuesday Comments:							
Wednesday Comments:							
Thursday Comments:							
Friday Comments:							
Saturday Comments:							
Sunday Comments:							

Additional observations:

Who impressed you with their skills? _____

Why? _____

Who did not impress you? _____

Why? _____

DELIVERY SKILLS
WEEKLY PRACTICE CHART

Week of: _____
Note where you practiced.

SKILL SETS PRACTICED

	Posture	Gestures	Eye Contact	Voice Volume	Inflection	Filler	
Monday Comments:							
Tuesday Comments:							
Wednesday Comments:							
Thursday Comments:							
Friday Comments:							
Saturday Comments:							
Sunday Comments:							

Additional observations:

Who impressed you with their skills? _____

Why? _____

Who did not impress you? _____

Why? _____

DELIVERY SKILLS
WEEKLY PRACTICE CHART

SKILL SETS PRACTICED

Week of: _____

Note where you practiced.

	Posture	Gestures	Eye Contact	Voice Volume	Inflection	Filler	
Monday Comments:							
Tuesday Comments:							
Wednesday Comments:							
Thursday Comments:							
Friday Comments:							
Saturday Comments:							
Sunday Comments:							

Additional observations:

Who impressed you with their skills? _____

Why? _____

Who did not impress you? _____

Why? _____

OBSERVATION SHEET

We learn a great deal from observing others. Analyze guests being interviewed on TV shows such as, *Meet the Press, This Week, Hardball, 20/20, O'Reilly Factor, Crossfire* and *60 Minutes*.

Show: Date:

Guest: Host:

Initial impression of guest: _____

Message was: Well defined / diluted / sidetracked

Why: _____

Write the first two words or sounds of the guest's answers:

_____   _____   _____

Physical presence
Fidgety? If so, how? _____

Were movements and gestures: Defined / limited / nebulous

Adjustments in chair: Frequent / noticeable / infrequent

Posture: Strong / passive / weak. Describe: _____

Eye contact: Sustained / fleeting.

Voice: Unwavering / cautious / hesitant

Filler used and frequency: _____

Did content dictate comfort level? _____

If so, how? _____

Rate the effectiveness of the guest (1 being disastrous and 10 being successful): _____

Overall observations: _____

OBSERVATION SHEET

We learn a great deal from observing others. Analyze guests being interviewed on TV shows such as, *Meet the Press, This Week, Hardball, 20/20, O'Reilly Factor, Crossfire* and *60 Minutes.*

Show: _____   Date: _____

Guest: _____   Host: _____

Initial impression of guest: _____

Message was: Well defined / diluted / sidetracked

Why: _____

Write the first two words or sounds of the guest's answers:

_____   _____   _____

Physical presence
Fidgety? If so, how? _____

Were movements and gestures: Defined / limited / nebulous

Adjustments in chair: Frequent / noticeable / infrequent

Posture: Strong / passive / weak. Describe: _____

Eye contact: Sustained / fleeting.

Voice: Unwavering / cautious / hesitant

Filler used and frequency: _____

Did content dictate comfort level? _____

If so, how? _____

Rate the effectiveness of the guest (1 being disastrous and 10 being successful): _____

Overall observations: _____

_____

PRESENTATION PREP SHEET

Presentation to: _____

Date: _____ Time: _____

What is the most important thing for your audience to remember?

_____

_____

STRUCTURING YOUR PRESENTATION

My objective (Mission, Purpose, Goal) is:

_____

_____

We are positioned as follows or the situation is as follows:

_____

_____

* * Ask if your understanding of the situation is correct.

The end result (Benefits, Consequences):

_____

_____

Next step:

_____

_____

Close with your Purpose Statement — "As you leave, I would like you to remember..."

_____

_____

OUTLINE

Opening – Objective: _____

_____

Body of Presentation

    Point #1:
    Support:

    Point #2:
    Support:

    Point #3:
    Support:

Summary: _____

_____

Purpose Statement: _____

_____

HELPFUL INFO TO REVIEW

Who will lead the presentation? _____

What are the roles of team members? _____

Who will attend? _____

A/V requirements: _____

Handouts: _____

Stories/Anecdotes: _____

Contact name and number: _____

PRESENTATION PREP SHEET

Presentation to: _____

Date: _____   **Time:** _____

What is the most important thing for your audience to remember?

_____

_____

STRUCTURING YOUR PRESENTATION

My objective (Mission, Purpose, Goal) is:

_____

_____

We are positioned as follows or the situation is as follows:

_____

_____

* * Ask if your understanding of the situation is correct.

The end result (Benefits, Consequences):

_____

_____

Next step:

_____

_____

Close with your Purpose Statement — "As you leave, I would like you to remember…"

_____

_____

OUTLINE

Opening – Objective: _____

_____

Body of Presentation

    Point #1:
    Support:

    Point #2:
    Support:

    Point #3:
    Support:

Summary: _____

_____

Purpose Statement: _____

_____

HELPFUL INFO TO REVIEW

Who will lead the presentation? _____

What are the roles of team members? _____

Who will attend? _____

A/V requirements: _____

Handouts: _____

Stories/Anecdotes: _____

Contact name and number: _____

PRESENTATION PREP SHEET

Presentation to: _____

Date: _____ **Time:** _____

What is the most important thing for your audience to remember?

_____

_____

STRUCTURING YOUR PRESENTATION

My objective (Mission, Purpose, Goal) is:

_____

_____

We are positioned as follows or the situation is as follows:

_____

_____

* * Ask if your understanding of the situation is correct.

The end result (Benefits, Consequences):

_____

_____

Next step:

_____

_____

Close with your Purpose Statement — "As you leave, I would like you to remember..."

_____

_____

Outline

Opening – Objective: _____

_____

Body of Presentation

    Point #1:
    Support:

    Point #2:
    Support:

    Point #3:
    Support:

Summary: _____

_____

Purpose Statement: _____

_____

Helpful Info to Review

Who will lead the presentation? _____

What are the roles of team members? _____

Who will attend? _____

A/V requirements: _____

Handouts: _____

Stories/Anecdotes: _____

Contact name and number: _____